*The English Gentleman's
Good Shooting Guide*

The English Gentleman's Good Shooting Guide

Douglas Sutherland

Illustrated by Alasdair Hilleary

Michael Joseph
LONDON

MICHAEL JOSEPH LTD

Published by the Penguin Group
27 Wrights Lane, London W8 5TZ, England
Viking Penguin Inc., 40 West 23rd Street, New York, New York 10010, USA
Penguin Books Australia Ltd, Ringwood, Victoria, Australia
Penguin Books Canada Ltd, 2801 John Street, Markham, Ontario, Canada
L3R 1B4
Penguin Books (NZ) Ltd, 182–190 Wairau Road, Auckland 10, New Zealand

Penguin Books Ltd, Registered Offices: Harmondsworth, Middlesex, England

First published 1989

Copyright © Douglas Sutherland 1989

Illustrations © Alasdair Hilleary 1989

Typeset in Monophoto $10\frac{1}{2}$ on 13pt Bembo
by Butler & Tanner Ltd.
Printed and bound in Great Britain
by Butler & Tanner Ltd
Frome and London
A CIP catalogue record for this book is available from the British Library

ISBN 0 7181 3313 7

To my sporting wife Diana

Contents

Join the Club

Today as never before in our island history we are suffering from problems of identity. Possibly this is due, like much else, to the curse of instantaneous communication and the consequent lack of privacy in our lives. Or then again, perhaps we do not communicate enough.

Whatever the reason we are very far removed from the spacious times when Queen Victoria sat securely on the throne. Then there was a place in society for everyone and everyone knew their place. Today there is a mobility which many people find alarming and they react by trying to affix labels of identity on everyone such as lower, lower middle, middle, upper middle, upper and stratospherically upper which far outdoes anything the class conscious Victorians sought to impose.

The closer one gets to the apex of the social triangle, the more insistent appears to be the need for an exactness of identity and this in turn has led increasingly to 'definition by sets'. This classification into sets has always been something the upper classes delight in. At the end of the last century, it was all the go to be considered part of the Sandringham set who clustered round the Prince of Wales. Then there were the party political but mostly society sets, like Londonderry House and the other lot at Cliveden.

Now the fashion is to seek to identify as belonging to a set grouped round some form of activity like polo or skiing or even such less clearly defined activity as simply spending most of one's time in nightclubs, oddly called Café Society.

Of all these what is generically referred to as the 'hunting, fishing and shooting' set is the one most generally held up to derision and scorn by the anti-everythings and regarded by others as the most exclusive and therefore the one with which it is the most desirable to identify with.

The task is not an easy one. They are an elusive breed to try and pin to the dissecting board, and one whose mannerisms and almost tribal customs are hard to define or adapt to with any great degree of authenticity. It is the same sort of difficulty as that which the average foreigner experiences, however familiar he may feel himself to be with the English language and English customs.

Who, for instance, cannot but sympathise with the anglophile shooting guest from the Continent who was advised by his host of the desirability of an early start to the next day's sport.

'We are having dinner early,' he told him, adding considerately, that he might feel like an early night.

'As you English say "early to bed and up with the cock!"' his guest replied with equal understanding.

The way of life of the country gentleman born and bred to enjoy the peculiar pursuits of the countryside is indeed far removed from that of many of his city cousins who, although they instinctively envy him what they may believe to be his more gracious and leisured life style, do not always fully appreciate just what hardships it can entail. Should, for example, his manservant when drawing the bedroom curtains remark that it would appear to be a splendid morning, he will feel the adrenaline stir in much the same way as will the city-bound gentleman anticipating a brisk day of business in his counting-house. 'Sun shining eh? I think I'll just grab a quick cup of coffee and go out and kill something,' he is likely to cry, before bouncing out of bed and reaching for his shot-gun.

This is the first of a series of three slim volumes designed to let these whose wish it is to identify with the hunting, shooting and fishing set know just what they may be letting themselves in for.

1

Pick your Bird

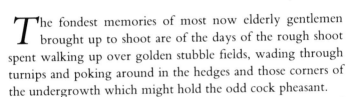

The fondest memories of most now elderly gentlemen brought up to shoot are of the days of the rough shoot spent walking up over golden stubble fields, wading through turnips and poking around in the hedges and those corners of the undergrowth which might hold the odd cock pheasant.

Now that has all gone in the wake of mechanised and chemicalised farming. Golden stubbles are a thing of the past and there do not even seem to be many turnip fields any more.

Shooting itself has become a much more formalised affair, which is natural enough when most people have to pack a whole leisurely shooting season into a few short, frantic days. This leads in turn to an involuntary form of specialisation. He is a lucky man indeed who can look forward with equal enthusiasm and excitement to the first day out on the moors and the successive opening days of the partridge and pheasant seasons. Each have their own individual charms but there are few today who can have the opportunity of enjoying them all in turn.

It might be worth, therefore, devoting a few pages to describing the other man's idea of heaven.

Grouse Shooting

The most holy day in the sporting calendar is 12th August. It is known even to those who have never held a gun in their hands as the Glorious Twelfth. It is the day which marks the opening of the grouse shooting season.

That the Twelfth has come to enjoy a special place in the heart of the nation, the equivalent perhaps of Bastille Day in France or Independence Day in America, is not, however, because it marks an event of great historical importance in the nation's history. It commemorates a social rather than a bloody revolution.

It was Queen Victoria who, with her obsessive love of all things Scottish, started it all. Scarcely had the first block of granite been hewn to build a new Balmoral than all Society with a capital 'S' were undertaking the long and uncomfortable trek northwards to spend a month or so in cold castles until convention permitted that they could return to their natural habitat in the jungles of Mayfair and Belgravia. The custom has survived both the building of a memorial to Prince Albert in Kensington Gardens and the death of Queen Victoria herself.

It might be said that this is a tribute to the enduring qualities of Lagopus Scoticus, the Scottish red grouse which is considered by many to be the ultimate sporting challenge for shooting men from all over the world. It is, however, the reverence in which the date is held in the eyes of High Society which remains the most powerful reason for its survival. Indeed the social nimbus which has come to surround the annual pilgrimage for the ritual slaughter of grouse on the rain-swept mountainsides of the Scottish Highlands, makes it so compulsive amongst some elements of the very rich that they simply cannot afford the stigma of being seen anywhere south of the Tweed after the end of Goodwood Race Week.

The best grouse moors are still, as they always have been, in counties like Yorkshire and Lancashire in the North of England but let that pass. It is the 'Scottishness' of grouse shooting which really counts when the chips are down.

Times have, however, considerably changed from what they used to be in what have now come to be thought of as the 'good old days' of the earth closet and the paraffin lamp. Then, for example, everybody went north for the shooting by train. There are few elderly sportsmen of the old school who do not still snuffle nostalgically about the departure platform at King's Cross Station on the eve of the Twelfth and remember the dogs salivating at the mouth whilst they towed their masters to their first-class sleepers, followed by an army of respectful porters, pulling behind them trolleys piled high with gun cases, cartridge boxes and all the paraphernalia needed for survival on the far frontiers, whilst in the restaurant car the attendants gave an extra special polish to the wine glasses, in anticipation of the rewards of the patronage of 'the milords'.

That was before the nationalisation of the railways and when everybody knew their own station – literally. The London North Eastern Railway which ran out of King's Cross was the line for gentlemen travelling up to the City of Edinburgh and then venturing further north to Aberdeen and Inverness to stay with the Scottish lairds on their Highland estates. Its rival, the London Midland Scottish, had to be content by and large with businessmen who carried briefcases with affairs to transact in Midland towns like Birmingham and Manchester before they carried on to, of all places, Glasgow. Nobody who was anybody went to Glasgow in those not-so-long-ago days.

Now everything is quite different.

Before the war the Highland laird who found a rich American to take his moor was regarded with envy by the other owners of vast acreages of otherwise unproductive heather and hill. It often made all the difference in paying the children's school fees and having something over for the plum pudding and crackers at Christmas. Today the American millionaire is no longer the legendary figure, representing the ultimate in the extravagance of wealth, which he used to be. Now it is the French and the Dutch, closely followed by the Germans, the Spanish and the Italians, who lead the annual gold rush for the hills and demand far exceeds supply.

Sharp-eyed businessmen look after what has become a multi-million-pound business and it is only the very richest of the rich amongst the owners of Highland estates who can afford the luxury of the odd day in the butts with a party of their own friends. Commercialism has them all by the throat and by and large it is an experience which even the most old-fashioned of lairds is finding hugely enjoyable.

There was a time too when, after the day's bag was brought down from the hill, the whole household would be put to packing the birds in those brown cardboard boxes with ventilating holes on the side and dispatching them on the night train to Auntie Mary and Cousin Agatha and the great host of friends and relations who expected to be remembered and receive their birds in places like Bournemouth or Bognor Regis the following morning. It was often an agonising business. 'Oh dear, there are only old birds left and we haven't sent to Uncle Bertie.'

'He won't notice. He's blind as a bat and gaga to boot.' The only really unforgivable sin was the sin of omission from the list.

Today the birds have hardly hit the heather before they are rushed off to the game dealer and even the guns are lucky if they get a brace to take home with them. The ballyhoo surrounding the jetting of the first birds down to London and even New York to be served for luncheon in the grandest hotels is exceeded in absurdity only by that other annual race to get the newly-born French Beaujolais across the Channel on the first day of the vintage.

A publicity-seeking Duke has been photographed crawling up a hillside at dawn to bag a grouse for instant dispatch to grace the hotel table of some anonymous but mega-rich businessman still sound asleep in his bed somewhere in Surrey. One very grand luxury hotel in Scotland, Gleneagles, had their head chef in his aprons pictured descending from a mountain by hang-glider with a grouse in his teeth. 'I'd rather he spent more time at his stove looking after the potatoes,' one disgruntled hotel guest was heard to remark at the time.

Vive le sport.

Pheasants

The pheasant shooting season opens on the 1st October. It is a date in the shooting calendar which goes totally unremarked. There are none of the hosannas which surround the 12th August when not to be out on the moor on the first day of the grouse shooting is to spell social ruin. To organise a pheasant shoot for the opening day would constitute a social *gaucherie* of the worst sort. Nobody would dream of having a proper day until the leaf is off the tree, which according to the caprices of our English weather can be reckoned as late October or more usually sometime in November.

There is a practical reason for this. It is simply that, with the trees in full fig, it is almost impossible to get the driven birds up in the air to present a sporting target rather than fluttering out of the undergrowth and knocking your hat off.

The whole business of shooting pheasants differs in another important respect from shooting grouse. It is that pheasants can be bred in captivity and released into the wild to build up stocks whilst grouse cannot. Thus the moor owner who fails to show his guests, paying or otherwise, a great number of birds can be excused on the grounds of too wet a spring, not enough snow, tick, worm or any other of the multitude of diseases and misfortunes which afflict the red grouse in the breeding season. The only excuse for not having enough pheasants to shoot at is that the host has been too mean to 'put down' sufficient birds to put up. So, in these commercial times, to let or hire a gun in a syndicate shoot is as much a business transaction with much the same predictability as the buying and selling of whatever it is that City tycoons trade in, the mysterious world of high finance.

Whilst this should in no way detract from the enjoyment of shooting as a sport it can be distracting when a gun takes out his pocket calculator after each drive to work out whether he has shown a profit or a loss.

Partridges

Whereas the breeding of pheasants with which to stock a shoot has been long established, the art of rearing partridges for the same purpose has only been mastered in comparatively recent years. From a peak in the years following the last war when the partridge population throve mightily leading to a record bag of 2,015 shot in Lincolnshire in 1952, numbers declined drastically until, with the increasing use of insecticides, the clearing of hedgerows and combine harvesting, they almost disappeared from the scene.

The same fate would have overtaken the pheasant had it not been for the efforts of the game farmers who breed them in ever increasing numbers to be driven over the guns each year and leave enough over to make it one of the commonest birds in the countryside. This pokes a decidedly tarry stick in the eye of the fanatical anti-blood sports, conservationist lobby.

Now the partridge is staging a comeback partly through its ability to adapt to changing conditions but largely because an effective method of putting down birds has been devised and astonishingly large bags are being reported again.

Unlike any other of our indigenous game birds there are two distinct breeds of partridge with totally different characteristics. They are the English partridge and the French Red Leg, known in shooting circles as 'Frenchmen' or 'Frogs'. Although the latter are rapidly gaining ground numerically and becoming more widespread geographically, they are the less highly regarded of the two by sportsmen. This is on account of their deplorable habit when driven of keeping sneakingly close to the ground and popping over the line of guns when least expected. It is in striking contrast to the English partridge who gets well up in the air where he can be seen and offers a far more sporting chance of getting killed. This is just another thing in the eyes of many fair-minded people which the French have to answer for.

Various

To browse through an old game book, one of the most highly prized possessions of any shooting man, has the same sort of fascination as those old-style stamp albums which devoted generous space for such now forgotten geographical anachronisms as Herzegovina, Bosnia or the Malay States. Including columns devoted to a record of such now comparatively rare additions to the game larder as the capercailzie and the ptarmigan, it is hard to imagine anything left over to put in the last column before the space for remarks, by tradition devoted to 'various'. It is with some dismay that I observe that those sumptuously-bound productions now available in all the top shops which purvey these sort of things no longer contain such exotica and space is rarely provided even for much more mundane entries such as rabbits and hares. How dreadfully dull not to have space to record additions to the bag of not-so-rare species like duck, snipe, woodcock or even such now apparently despised species as the woodpigeon!

Shooting pigeons coming into roost in a high wind tries the skill of even the deadliest of shots and surely flighting duck into a pond on a moonlit night must rate as one of the more exciting experiences for any devotee of the art.

Of all the birds now lumped together in the various column, none has quite the mystique of the woodcock. To kill a pair of woodcock, one with the right barrel and the other with the left, has always been considered a rare enough achievement to be talked about for a long time afterwards and there was certainly at one home a firm of purveyors of high-class spirits who offered a generous award of a bottle of their product for any authenticated report of the feat.

The woodcock also has the distinction of being the one bird of which it is permitted in even the best circles to adorn the person with its feathers as a mark of distinction. The practice, particularly amongst foreigners, of covering themselves with trophies of the chase from bristly things in their hatbands to fishing flies in the lapels of their jackets is one that is generally frowned on in this country. Even neckties with a motif of flying pheasants and such things as leaping salmon on the bonnets of motor cars are not really considered quite *comme il faut* by the English gentleman.

Quite why the tiny blue pin feathers of the woodcock, sported discreetly in the hat band of even the most formal of headwear of the city gent, should be a single exception, I do not know but there it is.

Perhaps it is a tiny act of revolution against the conformity which threatens to engulf us all.

Wildfowling

People who go wildfowling generally regard themselves as a different breed from the run-of-the mill shooting man. They tend to pursue their sport in unsociable hours, getting out of their beds in the smallest of small hours in order to be in a position behind some sea-wall or up to their middle in marsh-water by the time whatever it is they are shooting is beginning to get on the move.

There are few of the breed who can refrain from boasting of just how freezingly cold and generally appalling the conditions had been when they managed to bring down the odd goose or a couple of duck or of a morning when a suddenly rising wind had caused them only narrowly to escape from drowning.

All in all wildfowling is a rather specialist form of shooting which need not be gone into here in too much detail.

2

Getting Equipped

I THE RIGHT GUN

*T*here is a tradition handed down from generation to generation that the things one should never lend, even to a friend, are one's gun, one's horse and one's wife in that order. Although values may have changed in more recent times it is true to say that his gun still remains one of a gentleman's most valued possessions. It will in all probability have been inherited or bought for him by his father for some important occasion, like his eighteenth birthday.

His attachment to his gun has nothing to do with its efficiency or owe anything to the prestige of the name of its maker. In fact there are quite a few gentlemen of the old school who still shoot with hammer guns, or guns where the barrels have worn so thin with wear over the years as to be long 'out of proof' and come into the category of dangerous weapons.

Nor does he take pride in any prestige attached to the name of the maker. It is quite likely that his gun will date from the days when most country towns boasted a local gunmaker who made his own guns just as they had bakers who baked their own bread and butchers who killed their own meat. Traditionally they received the patronage of the local landowning families and it was only the grandees and the exceptionally rich who took their business to fashionable gunmakers in London, a few of whom like Messrs Purdey and Holland & Holland survive today to make guns for anyone who can afford the high price they charge.

All of which is not very helpful to anyone seeking advice on what sort of gun he should acquire when first purchasing one. Ask the average gentleman what make of gun he favours and he will look amazed at the question rather as if he had been asked if his wife wore knickers. It would be just something he had never given any thought to. And to try and find out for oneself by peering at the name engraved discreetly on the barrels is not really done, and rather like turning your fork over at a dinner party to see if it has the silver hallmark.

The easy way out if you are very rich is simply to put yourself on the waiting list with one of the top gunmakers, wait up to three years and you will have one of the most beautiful guns in the world. Whilst you are about it, order a matching pair. They will cost only slightly less than buying a grouse moor which is another nice thing to own. There is also the thought that when they pass down to the next generation your heirs can join the great majority who inherit a gun and be equally indifferent to any special social status it may be thought to confer.

More practical advice is to find something you like second-hand at a gun dealers and preferably one of those old established shops which used to make their own guns and which smell deliciously of linseed oil and wet mackintosh.

You can also do a lot worse if you want to buy a new gun than to get one made in Spain where they have a long tradition of making fine guns. Toledo steel used to have almost a monopoly of the market in the days when gentlemen were principally concerned with what sort of sword they should buy and, with the highly ornamental Damascus inlay so favoured by Spanish craftsmen, makes very elegant guns. They also shoot just as straight as any if the chap pulling the trigger has it pointed in the right direction.

An important thing to bear in mind when buying a gun is that you should never make a final decision until you have tried it out first. To be expected to do so would be as unreasonable as to buy a pair of shoes without trying them on.

By the same analogy to have a gun specially made for you is much the same as having a suit made instead of buying one off the peg. There are endless fittings to adjust the stock to the length of your arm and accommodate any other of your physical peculiarities.

Try your gun out at one of those shooting schools which are to be found up and down the country or better still take it for a day or two to a proper shoot. There are many opinions on the optimum length for the gun barrel and this can vary by quite a lot from the exceptionally short twenty-six inches to as long as an old-fashioned thirty inches. It finally boils down to what you feel most comfortable with.

Whilst on the subject of barrels it should perhaps be mentioned that these should be placed side by side, not one on top of the other in the style favoured on the other side of the Atlantic, where they are also apt to fit them with a gangster-type magazine which can be loaded with up to five cartridges. 'Over and Under' guns, as they as called, are commonly used here by the semi-professional on the clay pigeon shooting circuit and I have no doubt they are ideal for the purpose.

You will not, however, be voted the most popular boy in the class if you turn up with one next time you are invited to shoot at Sandringham.

★　★　★

Other Paraphernalia

Although his gun is the single most important item amongst the gentleman's sporting gear, there are all kinds of other impedimenta which he is apt to accumulate, only some of which are essential.

He will need, for example, in addition to a properly fitted gun case in which to transport his gun, a leather or canvas sleeve which has a strap so that he can carry his gun, protected from the rain or other vagaries of the weather, when walking to the next stand or line of butts. This is a comparatively modern practice. In more spacious and better organised times his gun would of course have been taken from him by his man at the end of each drive and handed back to him at the beginning of the next.

The same do-it-yourself principles also now apply to the problem of carrying your own cartridges. Most people now carry ammunition for immediate use in a cartridge belt, strapped round their middles. Others stick to the more old-fashioned cartridge bag slung over the shoulder. Either way, if there is plenty to shoot at, a reserve supply of cartridges has to be established to replenish stocks from time to time. It is a good piece of one-upmanship to own a stout leather box carrying upwards of five hundred cartridges, personalised with your initials embossed in black letters. It does no harm to have old P & O steamship labels or the odd air-freight sticker gummed on to establish the owner's international credentials.

If you take your own dog to a shoot it is important that it should be fitted with a proper leather collar and, by such small details as the type of clip on the leash, not display the amateurism of the owner. Only a quick release claw clip should be used; never the sort of side-spring clip usually favoured by owners who exercise their dogs in public parks. A whistle, or even more regrettably sometimes several whistles, slung round the neck are not always convincing evidence of an owner's authority over his dog. Those whistles with a pitch so high that only the dog is supposed to be able to hear it are particularly unimpressive. A good old-fashioned bellow is something most dogs are more likely to understand.

The carrying of weapons such as sheath knives or other side-arms so often favoured by foreigners is generally regarded as very unBritish.

In short, the less the enthusiastic sportsman resembles a Christmas Tree and the more a gentleman out for a stroll, the better.

II THE RIGHT DOG

There is a generally held belief – although only, let it be said, amongst the British – that the dog is man's best friend. It is a friendship which amounts in many cases to an obsessional love. It is, however, an obsession which takes many forms. The dog owners who groom their loved ones in order to parade them in the show rings, painting their toenails and curling their eyelashes, are quite a different species from the owner who keeps shooting-dogs.

There are those who keep shooting-dogs for sporting reasons and those who keep sporting-type dogs because they want the neighbours to think they are the sort of people who shoot. The latter usually treat their dogs in a manner which ensures that they develop acute neurosis and die at an early age from fatty degeneration of the heart. They are to be seen in various stages of their decline being taken for sedate walks on a lead in city parks or sitting gazing dolefully out of the windows of motor cars parked in suburban high streets waiting for the pubs to shut.

The relationship between a working dog and its owner is

totally different. Owners of gun dogs may have just as much affection for their animals as any other dog owners. It is only that they have a different way of showing it, often beating them to within an inch of their lives should they be so disobedient as to pursue their natural instincts by chasing a rabbit and keeping them confined in an outside kennel when they are not required to take part in various sporting activities. It is also general practice to have them sent away, during the most formative time of their lives, to be properly trained, rather after the fashion in which most gentlemen send their children off to boarding schools to learn the facts of life.

It is only when a shooting man's dog is nearing the end of its useful life and suffering acute arthritis from constant exposure that it will be allowed in the house. Then it will be given the undisputed right to occupy the best chair in the room, from which point of vantage it will growl menacingly at any stranger who might have the temerity to approach it. It will also be most likely that it will take to sleeping on the master's bed which, as at this stage in a working dog's life it inevitably smells of blocked drains, does not always appeal to the gentlemen's wife should she still happen to be sharing the marital couch.

Types of Sporting Dog

Undoubtedly the most popular shooting dog is the labrador. They come in two colours, black and varying shades of yellow. It is particularly important when buying a labrador for working purposes to make sure that it comes from a good working strain. Some years ago the professional dog breeders took up breeding the yellow ones (often called golden labradors) for the show ring and in consequence nearly ruined them as a working strain. It is only recently that they have started to stage a comeback as gun dogs.

One of the best working strains are the Sandringham labradors, originally from the Royal kennels. Don't think, however, if your puppy has a Sandringham Something-or-other in its pedigree that you have a near relation of the Queen's. The Sandringham dogs have been busily procreating since quite a long time now, rather like the Pilgrim Fathers to whom so many Americans are related.

Labradors are bred mainly as retrievers. The role of a well trained labrador is to sit behind its master when standing for driven birds or trot at his heels when walking up and only to leave his side when told to go and pick up a bird he has shot and bring it back whole, without making a meal of it first. If it can sometimes bring back a bird shot by somebody else and lay it at his master's feet as one of his, most owners will not be too angry with it and quietly add it to his own score for the drive.

There are many other breeds of gun dog with specialist skills bred into them over many generations. There are cocker spaniels whose traditional role is to hunt out game, pointers and setters to alert the walking-up gun to sitting birds, and springer spaniels to 'spring' them to order. There are breeds which are particularly adept at retrieving birds which have fallen in the water and others which excel at quartering in a turnip field.

Alas, now that shooting is confined largely to being a matter of standing still and waiting for the birds to be driven over the heads of the guns and rough shooting is becoming a thing of the past, these specialist skills in breeds, each of which used to have their ardent devotees amongst sportsmen, are no longer so highly prized.

This may be of some comfort to the large number of proud dog owners who maintain great prowess in the field for their own pets, be they pekinese descended from the brave hunting dogs of the ancient Chinese Emperors or any sort of mongrel whose mother can claim to have had a passing affair with one of the more orthodox shooting strains when the attention of its owner had been temporarily distracted.

There is also the example of Jemmy Hirst, a self-made man of great wealth who managed to train a large middle-white sow into becoming a most effective retriever of game he shot on his Yorkshire estates. That he was also accepted in hunting circles where he rode to hounds on the back of a bull only goes to show, even in those days, that imperfections of pedigree were not necessarily a bar to the social acceptance of both dog and master.

On the whole, however, anyone seeking acceptance amongst his fellow sportsmen in these less tolerant times is advised to play it safe and acquire a dog which would not be blackballed for membership of the Kennel Club.

Dog Training

Basically it is no more difficult for anyone to train a dog for the gun that it is to train a dog for anything else like fetching slippers or collecting the morning paper from the corner shop. A well bred game dog should do whatever it is required to do by instinct and to train it is largely a matter of breaking it from bad habits. The most cardinal sin a dog can commit on an organised shoot, and particularly walking up, is 'running in' and so putting up the game long before they are within shot of the guns.

There are all manner of home-made devices and much handed-down lore to help the do-it-yourself dog trainer. There is one device commonly used to stop a dog running in called a break-lead. This is a long lead attached to the dog's collar which allows it to run in so far until the lead is checked and pulls it up short. In practice the lead is often of sufficient length to allow the dog to get into a full gallop before being checked so that it turns a spectacular cartwheel.

Another old-fashioned remedy to bring a dog which is a bit wild into line is to load a shot-gun cartridge with grains of rice in place of shot and, when it sets off after a rabbit, give it a sharp reminder in the backside. Rice pellets sting extremely painfully which results in yelps of agonised protest and it is to be hoped better manners next time.

There was an occasion when a gentleman tried out this remedy on his dog which duly reacted in a highly theatrical manner and took off howling in protest. Unfortunately, a Frenchman further up the line, observing this bit of over-acting, took careful aim and bowled the dog over, killing it stone dead.

'Aha!' he cried to the astonished owner of the dog, 'I 'ave, as you English say, wiped your eye!'

Taken by and large, it is now generally considered a safer bet to send your dog to a keeper and risk losing touch with it during the most formative time in its life.

Other Dogs

Whilst a shooting man has a special relationship, as has been remarked, with his sporting dogs, there are other breeds of dog which are permitted a much greater degree of domestic intimacy in his household and which he holds in affectionate regard even if, as is often the case, they belong officially to his wife.

Amongst those held in highest favour are Jack Russell terriers so beloved by the fox-hunting fraternity for their traditional skill in digging out foxes which have gone to earth. They are jolly little dogs which come in all shapes and an infinite variety of colouring but mostly white, splotched in varying degrees with brown or black patches. They have the enviable distinction of not being recognised as a separated breed of dog at all.

The Jack Russell is regarded by professionals in the dog breeding business as to be so lacking in class as to be barred from entry to the annual dog show at Crufts lest they lower the tone of aristocratic exclusivity which they are so anxious to engender. This is something which is held by many to be greatly in the Jack Russell's favour. Those who own Jack Russell terriers often have quite a few of them so that it is difficult to avoid sitting on one of them when calling and, in consequence, getting bitten on the bottom. They also quite often bite small children.

The larger breeds of dog, like Alsations, Dobermann pinschers or Great Danes are not highly regarded as additions to a gentleman's household, however much their size may be considered to confer status on the less socially secure.

Gentlemen's wives in particular are apt to go dotty about very small breeds like the Pekinese and even the Chihuahua which their husbands make a great business of affecting to despise or at least view with amused tolerance. None the less, it is usually the husbands who finish up wiping their noses and generally tending to their other less mentionable needs.

Dachshunds have a particular aptitude for endearing themselves to him to the extent of him having them legally adopted in the event of a breakdown in marriage.

Corgis are one of the exceptions to the small dog syndrome, particularly when they reach pack proportions as has happened in the case of at least one owner who is otherwise held in the highest social regard.

★   ★   ★

III THE RIGHT CLOTHES

As I have remarked in an earlier work on the life style of the English gentleman,★ nothing gives away a man's standing as a gentleman so much as his clothes. In the same volume I recounted the story of a gentleman who was accosted by a friend whilst walking along Piccadilly in clothes which were well below the best sartorial standards.

'It does not matter how I dress in London,' he claimed. 'Nobody here knows me.'

Later the same friend visited him in the country where his clothes were no better.

'It does not matter how I dress here,' he said. 'Everybody knows me.'

Although these may seem to be observations which do not reconcile one with the other, they are none the less both true. The clothes he wears do stamp the gentleman in an almost indefinable way as belonging to the breed. At the same time this is not a consciously achieved effect and he really does not give a toss about the finer points of fashion or by his turnout try to impress his gentlemanliness on anyone.

This is doubly true when it comes to a question of dressing suitably for a day when out shooting. Nor is it a contradiction to claim that the harder it is tried consciously to emulate the nonchalant look, the less likely it is to be successfully achieved. This is really because it is not what you wear but how you wear it that counts.

At a gathering of city-suited gentlemen dressed for a business or social occasion be it in a Belgravia drawing room, the board-room suite in a New York Hotel or any other venue favoured by the international jet set, it would be hard to tell one national-ity from another and harder still to make any finer distinctions

★ *The English Gentleman*, Debrett Peerage Ltd, 1978

of class or caste. Parade a similar group on a Scottish hillside or on the lawn of a stately home in darkest Hampshire dressed with the common purpose of killing something and the differences between them are much more immediately obvious. No foreigner, however hard he tries, can come within a very long way of identifying with the typical English gentleman dressed for the kill, even should he wish to do so. Many indeed, whether from a sense of national pride or from sheer bloody-mindedness, make no attempt at all, parading in an assortment of costumes from lederhosen and jagtkleider to the feathers, frills and furbelows favoured by the more hot-blooded Latin countries of the Mediterranean.

Of all the visitors from overseas who make regular pilgrimages to our sea-girt isles in pursuit of game none are more dead to our hallowed traditions in the matter of dress than our American cousins from across the Atlantic. Whilst some would appear to have strayed by mistake from their home-town baseball stadium still heavily padded for the game and wearing those immensely long-peaked caps to keep our English rain off their faces, others dress in the unmistakable traditions of the Wild West when bronco-busting was tops amongst outdoor sports. That they are also amongst the most welcome and enthusiastic of our guests does not alter the effect they have on British wildlife. Even such a straight-flying breed as the pheasant has been known to take the most eccentric action to avoid a direct confrontation with the all-American hunter.

The gentleman's attitude to the curious form of dress adopted by visitors to our shores is one of affectionate condescension. It is not a tolerance which is extended in the same generous spirit to their own countrymen. Although the slight distinction between what is accepted and what is objected to in the matter of dress is difficult if not impossible to define, the difference between a born gentleman and a camouflaged one is often embarrassingly obvious. It is largely a matter of attitude.

If, for example, a gentleman were to turn up at a shoot wearing the sort of hat one would normally expect to see worn by a mountain guide in the Austrian Tyrol, it might be regarded as an amusing eccentricity. If, however, a guest of whom it was only known that he was in advertising or 'something in the City' were to do so it would be immediately put down to his not knowing any better.

Hats can in fact take on a wide variety of form. One of the more traditional is the peaked cap which many gentlemen wear on almost every occasion, with perhaps the exception of Armistice Day parades or funerals. It is usually made of tweed and can be folded up and put in a jacket pocket. It is primarily a working gentleman's hat.

'What is your pleasure, sir?' the superior assistant in a classy department store asked of a rather bewildered looking customer.

'My pleasure is fornicating and flying pigeons,' he replied 'but a've cum in 'ere for a flat 'at.'

The working man's 'flat hat' is exactly the same type of hat. It is only that the working gentleman wears his in a distinctive way, pulled down over his nose after the manner of a guardsman's cheese-cutter. Many of those who try to imitate this style finish up looking like pigeon fanciers.

What is worn on the feet can also be a trap for the unwary. What a shooting gentleman wears when he goes out shooting is knee-length woollen stockings and a pair of stout leather shoes. Gumboots are very seldom worn. This is for the very practical reason that, when walking through wet turnips or other heavy undergrowth, gumboots fill up with water which the wearer has to squelch around in uncomfortably until he gets home some hours later. To stop and tip out the water and start again is an even more uncomfortable process. Gentlemen who go out shooting expect to get their feet wet and shoes dry out far more quickly and comfortably than gumboots. Those green wellies with little straps at the top which have become part of the uniform of Sloane Rangers (a fairly new invention in the social spectrum) have no advantage over ordinary gumboots. They only draw attention to the wearer's anxiety about not getting his feet wet, even on the dryest of days with the going firm, at the local point-to-point.

Protection against the wet has, in fact, never been something which worries the average gentleman very much. A garment called a raincoat has never had a place in his wardrobe. If he has an umbrella, it will be kept tightly rolled and only carried on formal occasions. If he were ever to unroll it moths would, in all probability, fly out and in any case, as many gentlemen no longer can afford to keep a batman or a valet, he has no one who knows how to roll it up neatly again.

He will, however, have a great number of jackets. He will have a jacket which he wears out shooting and may or may not match his nether garments, be they knee-breeches or what used to be called plus-fours. He will also have gardening jackets, a hunting jacket, a dinner jacket and so on. The dinner jacket should match his trousers but is never referred to as a dinner suit. Jackets are never referred to as sports jackets without referring to the sport for which they are intended to be worn. Nor is he a great user of those sorts of blazers which have a badge emblazoned on the handkerchief pocket, indicating that he is a member of some sort of club or association.

A good general principle is to concentrate on getting the head and the feet looking right and what happens in between does not matter overmuch.

★ ★ ★

IV   THE RIGHT CAR

Cars, like most other things mechanical, are not something of which the average gentleman has a deep understanding. He will get extremely angry with them if they cease, for any reason, to work, often resorting to kicking them petulantly. He will only have them washed and generally looked after if he has somebody else to do it for him and invariably forgets to replace the petrol cap if he has to fill up the tank himself at one of those self-service petrol stations which now seem to be everywhere.

After making allowance for this general indifference, it is also true to say that when purchasing a vehicle he does try to make sure, by asking the opinion of anyone within earshot, that what he is buying is capable of doing what he needs it to do as efficiently and economically as possible and without too much supervision. This applies in particular to any vehicle which is not required simply to drive up to London, visit friends or for his wife to drive down to the village. For this latter purpose almost anything will serve. For himself he is not a great buyer of flashy cars and regards anyone he sees driving a car like a Rolls-Royce with the greatest suspicion.

One of his main requirements for a car is that it can be driven across a field. When the Land Rover first appeared on the scene some years ago now, it had many of the attributes of the American Jeep which he had so taken to during the war and he greeted it with the greatest of enthusiasm as the ideal vehicle for his peacetime pursuits. By and large this still remains his view.

All the luxurious and elaborate variations on the theme which have since flooded the market have left him unimpressed. Fortunately for the various manufacturers, these have been snapped up by those conscious of their social image who use them for doing the shopping in the wilder parts of suburbia.

Over the years the sporting gentleman has made his own modifications in cases where his needs have not become standard fitments. The features which he regards as essential on an all-purpose vehicle are, reading from the front end:

A very strong get-out-of-my-way bumper bar in front. Sometimes this supports a long box with a lid which acts as an auxiliary carrier for game and which is convenient for throwing in such birds or ground game with which he might have come into involuntary contact whilst driving along country roads.

A compass, usually stuck to the windscreen, presumably for discovering in which direction he is pointing when driving across country which he knows like the back of his hand. This is pure conceit. He never has occasion to look at it which is just as well as it doesn't usually work.

A gun rack fitted across the width of the vehicle behind the driver's seat with room to carry up to six guns.

Two clips fitted on the outside of each side of the roof. These are to carry his rods, ready for use whenever he goes to fish on someone else's water. Where he has his own fishing these are usually kept in his fishing hut by the river and are never normally dismantled.

A wire-mesh grid fitted across the back to make a separate compartment or cage cut off from the rest of the interior. This is to confine the dogs or any children who cannot be relied upon to sit quietly in the passenger seats. It usually has bowls for drinking water, dry biscuits and other comforts.

A very large roof rack which covers the entire roof. This is mainly to carry hay bales.

A flap at the back which lets down to let out dogs and/or children when occasion demands. It also locks in a horizontal position and is most useful as a makeshift table for picnic lunches or for people to stand on to get a better view at point-to-points and similar occasions.

All vehicles must have, as standard fitments, a four-wheel-drive gear box with a special knob which puts it in low ratio. It also has a tow-bar fitment at the rear to pull anyone else who has had the folly to try and follow him across country, out of the ditch or whatever else (he hopes) they may finish up in. This is very good for his ego.

Gentlemen are very wary of having the sort of jokey stickers they see on the back of other people's cars when they drive on the motorway. They will only themselves display the names of causes in which they sincerely believe, such as the Royal Society for the Protection of Birds or the World Wildlife Fund.

Stickers urging support for one political party or another at election times are also considered by most to be bad form although less controversial party issues like 'Bring Back the Rope' may occasionally be given an airing.

3

The Sporting Wife

Nothing could be more varied than the roles the female of the species plays in the different worlds of hunting, shooting and fishing. In the hunting field and behind the carefully composed façade of those who have dedicated their lives to the often thankless task of keeping down foxes, there may be suspected to lurk a less selfless motive. As one elderly rustic leaning on a hayrake, briefly removing his clay pipe from his mouth, was heard to remark to his companion as the immaculately turned-out field streamed past, 'Sex maniacs, the lot of them!'

The scene on the river bank is a totally different one. When out fishing women are often referred to as the 'Unfair Sex' on account of their frequently succeeding, despite their almost total lack of either experience or skill, in catching more and bigger fish than their male counterparts. Unless they are prepared to admit, with a proper show of maidenly embarrassment, that this is entirely due to a fiendishly unfair share of good luck, it is something which often leads to rather less than that harmony which equality in sport is designed to foster.

In these respects the role of women when out shooting is far more honestly and clearly defined. She is seldom allowed to appear on terms of armed equality. Her role is a secondary one but its importance is recognised in the same way as the traditional role of the camp follower was long recognised in our proud military history.

The female auxiliaries are both hewers of wood and drawers of water but they are also the most fervent admirers of the prowess of their menfolk as well as their comforters when things do not go quite as well as expected.

It is generally accepted that ladies should not put in an appearance on the shooting scene until lunchtime. The day when a man could go off for a day's shooting with a few corned beef sandwiches in his jacket pocket and a flask of whisky has long since gone. Today we live in an age when the shooting lunch is the *sine qua non* of the day's sport and it is then, and not before, that the shooting wives and other female auxiliaries come into their own. It is their finest hour.

The ritual which is the shooting lunch should be closely examined by all those, both male and female, who wish to extract the maximum in terms of social advantage from a day in the field or on the hill.

On the very grandest shoots and particularly when grouse driving, which often takes place in remote places far removed from human habitation, shooting-huts may often have been specially built and equipped to provide shelter and comfort. In other cases, the front parlour of a keeper's cottage or other habitation is pressed into service with facilities for cooking huge pots of soup and stews which together with the Stilton cheese and digestive biscuits and many cases of wines and spirits, make up the basic necessities for the lunchtime break.

Traditionally the ladies arrive early so as to make sure that everything will be ready in plenty of time for the return of the hungry hunters. The large pots will be bubbling away, the drinks will have been set out, the port decanted on the sideboard and the room already smelling comfortably of wet tweeds and dry sherry by the time they put in an appearance.

Shooting lunches are the time for general bonhomie with remarks like, 'By Jove, that was a corker you brought down at the last drive!' which can be roughly translated as 'It was the only damned bird you hit all morning' or 'You were quite right to leave that one which went right over your head', meaning 'You never even saw it. Why don't you get your glasses cleaned?'

Everyone speaks in very loud voices which may be because most of them are suffering from gun deafness but, more probably, because they have forgotten to take out their earplugs. Incidentally, earplugs are a comparatively new idea and seldom worn by gentlemen of the old school which is why so many of them are permanently deaf in the left ear.

During the lunch hour there is a sort of defence mechanism which operates on the 'I won't tell on you if you don't tell on me' principle. After all, they still have all the afternoon to get through. The time for the post mortems will come later when most of the less popular guns will have gone home.

Apart from a general supervisory role on the part of the ladies, coordinated by the hostess or senior wife, their part is to express non-partisan admiration of their menfolk. It is also, when the bag is being laid out and counted by the head keeper, to refrain from tactless remarks like 'Who got that poor little hen pheasant then?' on a cocks-only day – unless it is clear that the offender is the man in the loud-check suit standing by himself and whose name nobody seems to remember.

It is after the port has been duly circulated and the beaters who have been stolidly munching their sandwiches outside in the rain have moved off to get into position to start the next drive that the real jockeying for position begins.

After lunch ladies may, if they should so wish, join the guns. That is to say, stand behind them during the drives in the role of admiring spectators. This is the time to throw their hats in the ring for it is not incumbent on them that wives should stand with their husbands and indeed it is not flattering to the other guns should they decide to do so unless they have been very recently married or become engaged to the gun in question.

This always seems to create a situation where, by some mysterious alchemy, most of the ladies present select the same gun on whom to bestow the favour of their presence. Unlike groupies at a pop concert, however, the rule is one lady to one gun. The result is that quite a lot of the bonhomie is apt to evaporate whilst they sort the matter out between themselves.

There are one or two exceptions to the rule that ladies should only make their first appearance at lunchtime. Whilst, as it has been explained, it is still regarded as unladylike, if not downright eccentric, to show any signs of being proficient with a gun, the same thing does not apply when it comes to handling a dog.

Some of the leading breeders of dogs are ladies and it is by no means unusual for them to handle their own dogs at gundog trials and other demonstrations of skill. There are also not a few ladies married to husbands who shoot who take to dog handling as a form of self defence. It gives them an independent entrée to a male-dominated world and they are greatly in demand at shooting parties on their own account. A woman with a reputation as 'a good picker-up' mixes with the men invited to shoot on equal terms; indeed there are many husbands with wives who have a talent in this direction, to whom they owe their invitation to shoot, despite their own reputation for being indifferent performers.

Ladies who are good at picking-up, that is to say who have a dog good at finding dead or wounded birds after a drive, have a distinct advantage over those ladies who only come up, as it were, with the rations.

The other role which ladies can perform on equal terms with men is to act as beaters. Beating – the act of driving the birds over the guns – can be a very exacting task. It entails walking many miles often through the roughest country, fighting through thick undergrowth, fording, and often falling into streams and hidden ditches whilst waving a large white flag tied to a long piece of stick and, at the same time, emitting wild and warlike cries.

A day 'at the beating' is a highly regarded perquisite amongst country folk. Beaters get paid upwards of ten pounds a day with, as often as not, a free bottle of beer to wash down their own sandwiches and sometimes the odd rabbit to take home for Sunday lunch.

Today it is not unknown for young ladies, anxious to impress a boy-friend numbered amongst the guns of her qualifications as a 'jolly good sport', to volunteer to have a go. They finish the day totally knackered but it is little a good hot bath and a couple of decent gin and tonics will not put right and often proves to have a strong aphrodisiac effect on the gentlemen in question.

There was a recent occasion on one of the more famous Perthshire moors when a young lady, who was a member of the house party which had rented the shooting, volunteered for a day with the beaters and who applied herself to the task with perhaps a greater degree of enthusiasm than was entirely necessary.

The day was a particularly hot one, the distances to be walked by the beaters unusually long and the terrain exceptionally precipitous. In the course of one arduous drive the young lady was so overcome by the heat of the sun and the energetic nature of her exertions that she first of all removed her outer garments and then more intimate ones until, by the time she came into view of the line of waiting guns, she was entirely naked from the waist up. Quite what effect this had on the guns is not related but the head keeper was heard to remark that she had 'fair skeer'd the burrds'.

All in all, ladies at shooting parties are required to pull their weight.

4

Deer Stalking

There was a time in Queen Victoria's day when the stalking of the Red Deer was the *ne plus ultra* in sport for many gentlemen. It had much of the challenge of man against the wild with the added attraction that it involved a great deal of arduous physical exercise, although Queen Victoria's son when Prince of Wales rather let the side down in this respect by having the deer driven to him so that he could shoot them at close range from a grouse butt with a shot-gun.

Physical challenge was the very stuff of life for the nineteenth-century sportsmen when the coming of a mechanical age was casting its long shadows and it represented a revolt against the foppishness of the Regency Bucks. They were forever betting that they could physically walk, run or ride faster or more furiously than the next man or that they could catch, kill or otherwise annihilate greater numbers of birds or beasts in a shorter time than anyone else.

Anything from shooting tigers in Bengal, climbing Swiss Alps to shoot chamois or sliding down them in two pieces of board, hunting wild boar or paddling up the Nile in search of crocodiles, made a welcome relief from the dreadful boredom

of being a well-off gentleman in an unprecedented period of peace interrupted only by some very minor wars.

In this context the stalking of the stag on the Scottish mountainsides was a mild enough business but at least it was better fun than attending those interminable levees and Highland balls which were so much part of doing the Scottish Season.

That today stalking, after a number of years in the doldrums, is once again becoming fashionable and 'a good thing to do' is an encouraging sign that a new generation is becoming increasingly disenchanted with the prospect of doing nothing more physical than making piles of money at an early age sitting in front of a computer. It at least takes the responsibility of keeping down the deer population from those of greater age whose legs are beginning to creak as well as putting up the blood pressure of the anti-blood sports lobby to a dangerously high level. This can't be a bad thing.

A Day on the Hill

To go deer stalking has glamorous connotations far beyond anything imaginable in a day out game shooting. To be invited for a day or a week's stalking and staying in a remote hunting lodge has about it a spine-tingling *frisson* of adventure and, particularly for the fairer of the two sexes, high overtones of somehow slightly dangerous romance, rather in the genre of Barbara Cartland.

The reality does not always come up to expectations. First of all there is the weather to contend with. Swirling mist and fog may have some excitement value in the opening chapters of a Gothic novel but it makes for rotten stalking weather. Torrential rain is worse, largely because there is a tradition amongst the devotees of stalking that bad weather conditions are no excuse for not setting out for the high peaks where

41

conditions are likely to be even more impossible. To settle down in front of a roaring log fire with a week-old copy of *The Times* in which somebody has already done the crossword and wait for the appearance of a non-existent sun over the yardarm to signal the moment for a first bash at the whisky bottle, which is the only alternative, is considered to be the worst of impossibly bad form.

Nor does a hot sun make a great deal of difference to the tribulations to which the dedicated stalker is heir. There are midges of the variety which have an insatiable thirst for blood matched only by the piranha fish.

Then there is the problem of clothing. Set out lightly clad and the weather will suddenly change. At the furthest point from human habitation it will start to snow steadily or a sharp frost will set in. Anticipate the worst and, by the time you have reached two thousand feet, the heat from the sun will be in excess of anything normally experienced in the Red Sea.

Dressing the Part

Although great store may be set by those anxious to show themselves off to the best advantage, there is always the limiting factor of practicability. This is a lesson which is more quickly learned halfway up a mountainside in mid-November than in the Royal Enclosure at Ascot in June.

There is a golden rule. Always wear leather on your feet and have a practical hat.

It might perhaps be remarked here that deer stalking, like fox hunting, is one of the few sports where women can compete on equal terms with men. It was not always so because one of the hangovers of Victorian prudery was to preclude the possibility of a lady of virtue finding herself alone, and beyond a call of help, with a man. Today, that a female should find herself in a Lady Chatterley situation with a rugged hill stalker must surely be one of the more appealing aspects of the sport in these emancipated days ... but to return to the matter of dressing the part.

There is an item of unisex headgear, called a 'deerstalker'. It is a hat with a peak fore and aft with flaps on either side which can, when not required, be fastened by a button on the crown. This is a particularly suitable hat when used for the original purpose for which it was designed. The idea is that, under rigorous weather conditions, the flaps can be undone and fastened under the chin, whereupon the whole thing becomes hopelessly uncomfortable and impracticable. Just the same, to wear a deerstalker with flaps which are only for show and which do not actually undo is almost as bad a social solecism as wearing a made-up bow tie. In all other respects it is ideal wear for the hill, offering both shade from the sun in front and protection from rain dripping down the back of the neck behind.

All other types of Sloane Ranger wear are taboo. Any sort of knee-length rubber boot and particularly anything with a rubber sole is an impossibility. So also are those otherwise very practical waterproof jackets with large pockets fastened with a press stud, known as Barbours (whoever Barbour was). These are highly practical for almost all other sorts of outdoor activity including shopping in Penge High Street but not much use when it comes to stalking. The reason is that they *crackle*. The red deer's only defences against its enemies are its acute sense of smell and hearing. Unless the stalker is dressed entirely in a rough tweed which does not crackle, he or she is at a considerable disadvantage.

★   ★   ★

The Stalk

It may seem trite to remark that the be-all and end-all of the stalk is the stalker. It cannot however be overemphasised. When Andrew Lang wrote:

> I am the batsman and the bat,
> I am the bowler and the ball,
> The umpire, the pavilion cat,
> The roller, the pitch, and stumps, and all.

he was quite obviously not thinking of a cricket match. He was thinking of a stalker on the hills of his homeland.

Stalkers come in the ratio of one stalker to one man with a rifle – or woman as the case may be. For the first-timer the initial meeting with the stalker into whose charge he or she is delivered is at least as momentous as any meeting between Mr Stanley and Dr Livingstone. He will eye his charge up and down noting points for and against with the experienced and slightly jaundiced eye of a horse dealer. It is most unlikely that, at a first meeting, he will indicate his approval. Do not be hurt. All that you can hope for is that you will grow on him.

Nor should anyone whose form with a rifle is an unknown quantity be insulted if asked to demonstrate that they know what they are about by firing a few shots at a target. A sporting rifle is about ten times more lethal than a shot-gun and fires a bullet which carries for great distances so it is important to know not only which end the bullet comes out of but that it is pointing in roughly the right direction when the trigger is pressed.

Once on the hill you are entirely under the command of your stalker. He is the captain of the ship and you are the crew. If he says crawl you crawl. If he says 'Keep your bloody bottom down' you keep your bloody bottom down.

It is one of the uncertainties of stalking that you never know when you set out just how long you are going to be out for. That is another thing that is up to the stalker. If he is any use he will have a very good idea where the 'beasties' will be. If the wind is in a direction which makes it impossible to get close enough to them for a shot, he might decide to abandon ship and you will be back in the shooting lodge again in plenty of time for lunch. On the other hand with everything set fair you might be out until dark and kill two or more 'beasties'.

In earlier days when rifles were fitted only with open sights shooting a deer was not nearly the precise science it has become since the introduction of telescopic sights. A good stalker should be able to get you to within a hundred yards of the beast he has selected for you and will not allow you to take the shot unless it is standing just right to give the best chance of making a clean kill. At that point, and not before, it is entirely up to you.

A stag can only be cleanly killed by a shot in the right part of the neck or behind the shoulder to the heart, which means hitting a target about the size of a saucer. You will not be popular if you miss and only wound the beast. It is the rule of the game that a wounded beast must be followed until it is finally put out of its misery, even if this means that you will miss the hot bath and very large whisky at the end of the day which you have been dreaming about since early on.

Going for Gold

Should it be your ambition, having successfully stalked and killed your stag, to have a fine set of antlers to have mounted and hung in the hall of your ancestral mansion, it is most likely that you will be disappointed. The days when sportsmen hankered to shoot a 'Royal' to display alongside the heads of everything from tigers to bison garnered from hunting expeditions to the far corners of the world, have long since passed. It is most likely that the stag you will have been allowed to shoot has a very poor head of antlers indeed with very few or no 'points' or branches on its horns. A beast with a poor head which really needs culling from the herd anyway is known as a 'switch' and has already been marked down as expendable. The classic head with twelve well balanced points is known as a Royal. Even rarer and therefore more desirable is an 'Imperial' which has fourteen or more points. With modern deer farming pampered deer are now growing enormous heads of antlers which when cast at the end of the season are sold at high prices to trophy hunters but this is not really considered to be quite the thing.

The Germans, the most assiduous trophy hunters in the world, claim the world's finest head to be a twenty-three pointer in the Maritzburg collection in East Germany although one of the thirty-three points was shot, in 1696, by the future King Fredrick I of Prussia. This also has always been regarded as overdoing it a bit.

The carcass of the deer you will have shot remains the property of the owner of the ground – known as a deer 'forest', although devoid of trees – and will be ceremoniously 'gralloched' by the stalker, i.e. have its entrails removed, before being taken down the hill, probably by pony, on its way to the dealer to whom he contracts the sale of his venison. It will then probably be shipped off to Germany where the demand for Scottish venison appears to be insatiable.

There are other by-products of the carcass of a stag which can provide a rich avenue for the deer farmer or owner of a deer forest. One of these is what is known as the 'velvet'. This is the fur-like covering on newly-grown antlers which is eventually rubbed off in the natural course of the stag's growth. This 'velvet' is highly prized in eastern countries for its aphrodisiac qualities.

So too is another part of the stag known as its pistle and

which is in fact its reproductive organ. Powdered pistles are claimed to have aphrodisiacal qualities of such extraordinary potency that rich merchants in countries like Laos will pay a king's ransom for a very small-sized tin.

5

Etiquette in the Field

The first ritual when all the guns are assembled at the beginning of the first drive is to draw for places. The place you draw is marked with a numbered peg – usually on a card stuck in a cleft stick – or by a number on your grouse butt which coincides with a number you will have drawn from a neat little leather case offered to you by your host. It is only on the most autocratic of shoots that the host places the guns after each drive so that the most important guns (which usually includes himself) always get the stands where they are likely to have the most shooting. The more democratic system of drawing for places is made more democratic still by the rule that the guns move on one, or more often two, places after each drive. Thus if you draw peg number one for the first drive, for the second drive you will be on peg three and so on.

The usual number of guns is either eight or nine. Particularly when there is an odd number of guns, there is often a dreadful outbreak of confusion because old Colonel Belch has left his adding machine behind and can't get his sums right – and anyway he has forgotten what his number was in the first place.

It is also not unusual on a pheasant shoot for there to be one or two walking guns. This is a role which is apt to fall on the younger members of the party on account of the decrepitude of some of the others. Walking guns either take their place in the line of beaters plunging through deep undergrowth or stroll more sedately on the flanks outside the wood which is being beaten. The job of the flanking gun is to take birds which try to break out. That is to say, any bird which shows a disinclination to fly forward over the guns and tries to sneak off in another direction. Walking on the flanks can be a very pleasant chore for those not totally crippled with arthritis and they are frequently rewarded with a lot of shooting. The lot of the inside walking guns is not generally so happy. The rule is that they should only shoot at birds doubling back over the beaters' heads. For anyone stumbling forward, being ripped to bits by thorns and stung on all exposed parts of the body by nettles, to bend over backwards to shoot a bird behind is a gymnastic feat which is not easy to learn.

To make matters worse, beaters are apt to be far more critical of a missed bird than even the most competitive of one's fellow guns. They are also much less inhibited in expressing their derision. Openly voiced comparison between a bird travelling at great speed and briefly glimpsed between the trees and a barn door are not uncommon.

When each drive is over it is customary for there to be a short break in the proceedings whilst the beaters regroup, the pickers-up go about their business and the guns stamp their feet and join together in small groups to discuss their successes and offer their congratulations. Missed shots should never be mentioned unless by the person who has done the missing and wishes to explain how a fly had got in his eye at the critical moment.

This is also the time when flasks start to make their appearance from back pockets, either for the owner to take a surreptitious swig or to be passed from hand to hand with much coughing and spluttering and wiping of moustaches. The most usual contents of the hip flask are either cherry brandy, sloe gin, malt whisky, Drambuie or various combinations thereof, frequently mixed with Crabbie's Ginger Wine as an extra insurance against a sudden cold snap in the weather.

Shooting parties vary greatly in degrees of conviviality. It is generally conceded that the biscuit in this respect is taken by those shoots in counties like Norfolk when two or three farmers are gathered together in the name of good neighbourliness and the day starts with a shooting breakfast where the kippers are cooked in gin and the coffee laced with brandy.

At the other end of the scale they can be much more sober affairs but it is generally considered a poor show if having the odd snort to keep the circulation going is looked upon with disfavour.

Particularly when shooting driven grouse, the waiting between drives is frequently quite lengthy. The beaters are often required to cover great areas of moorland to bring in the birds whereas for the guns it is sometimes simply a matter of turning round in their butts to face the birds being driven back over them from the opposite direction. This puts a heavy strain on anyone who might, for any reason, have signed a pledge to abstain from the consumption of alcohol.

One of the most unpopular characters to be met with when out shooting is the man who, the moment a drive is over, raises a clamour about the picking up of birds he claims to have shot. Like the resident bore in any decent club, most shoots are afflicted with one of the species.

No sooner has the whistle sounded which announces that the drive is over than he is dancing around bellowing for a keeper or one of the pickers to launch a search party for the birds he has killed which always seem to have fallen into the thickest bush or dropped – stone-dead, of course – somewhere in the middle distance. It is quite outside his comprehension that he should have had a clean miss so, in his logical mind, it follows that there must be a dead bird somewhere around for every shot that he has fired. The time and energy spent in searching for his frequently entirely mythical birds stretches the patience of all concerned to an infuriating degree but 'the-man-who-never-misses' remains unmoved and convinced that he is the victim of a conspiracy of dog handlers who own dogs that have no sense of scent. He never, incidentally, has a dog of his own.

The other well-known menace in the firing line is the man who 'poaches' the birds from his neighbouring guns. The worst offence is to take a bird which is clearly going to fly closer to the next man before he has had a chance himself of having a shot at it. Then to shout, 'Sorry, old man. Thought you hadn't seen it,' is only to aggravate the offence.

There was an occasion which is now recorded in the annals of a famous Aberdeenshire grouse moor where the host, now long since dead, was as noted for the irascibility of his temperament as he was for his fervent adherence to the Catholic Faith. One of his guests on the opening day of the grouse-shooting season happened to be the Bishop of Aberdeen who had the reputation of letting his gun off at everything in sight regardless of anyone who might have a prior claim. Whilst shooting in the next butt to his host, the Bishop started the day by taking one or two birds which a fair judge might have decreed to be rather more on the host's side of an invisible dividing line. Finally he transgressed too far when he neatly shot a bird almost at the end of his host's gun barrels.

This so infuriated the host that, completely forgetting the respect due to the Cloth, he immediately retaliated by removing a turf from the front of the Bishop's butt. This in turn so enraged His Grace that he replied by doing his host a similar favour. Thus whilst the grouse continued to stream overhead unnoticed, the two elderly gentlemen got down to serious hostilities blazing away at each other like two opposing sides in trench warfare. There is no knowing where it might have ended had not the Bishop's loader had the good sense to tie an off-white handkerchief to the end of his shooting stick and gingerly raise it above the parapet which the host took to be a sign of unconditional surrender.

Shooting with Two Guns

In the past it was not uncommon at big shoots for two and sometimes three guns to be used. For this reason the top gunmakers like Messrs Purdey customarily made guns for their customers as a matching pair, rather in the same way as, when ordering a suit from a West End tailor, he would always make it with two pairs of trousers unless told to the contrary. This is something people can rarely afford nowadays and indeed there are few shoots where the number of birds justifies the multiple use of weapons.

The art of shooting with two guns calls for great speed and skill in changing guns and it used to be said of the really top marksmen that they could shoot so fast as to have four dead birds in the air at the same time.

In the heyday of the battues at the turn of the century when the number of pheasants shot in a day were numbered in thousands rather than hundreds, the aristocracy of the shooting clique who clustered round the person of the Prince of Wales, later Edward VII, used to practise for the opening of the season with all the dedication of athletes training for the Olympics. It was said of Lord Ripon, a contender for the honour of being acclaimed the best shot in England, that, during the close season when there was nothing for him to kill, he would spend hours shooting at flies with paper pellets propelled by a tiny catapult to study how much he should aim off when shooting high pheasants.

His great rival, Lord Walsingham, would always excuse himself immediately after dinner on the eve of an important shoot on the grounds that he had a headache. He would then retire to his bedroom where he would spend hours with his loader practising changing guns.

In more recent times at a shoot held at one of our stateliest homes when the guests were expected to shoot with two guns, one of the party, to his great consternation, had his regular loader report sick on the morning of the great day. Bemoaning his misfortune over breakfast one of the young men who was a member of the house party but was not shooting that day volunteered to act as a stand in, blithely declaring that he had had a lot of experience of shooting with two guns.

On the first drive the sky was suddenly filled with birds and the gun took a neat right and left with his first two barrels but on passing over his first gun with his right hand and stretching over his left hand for the second gun whilst keeping his eyes fixed on high, he grasped nothing but air.

'What the hell happened!?' he shouted as the last pheasant disappeared over his head.

'I don't know about you, sir,' remarked the young man politely 'but I hit one and missed one.'

Further Misdemeanours

Apart from the importance of good manners when out shooting, there are certain other misdemeanours which you may commit and which will not contribute to your general popularity with the rest of your party.

The worst of these is swinging across the line; that is to say, continuing to swing your gun with the bird as you are taught to do at the shooting school and waiting until you are in line with the other guns before letting fly. This of course is doubly dangerous when shooting low-flying birds like partridges and grouse. It is common enough when shooting from a butt to find tall sticks on either side of the butt indicating the point beyond which it is dangerous, in your understandable excitement, to swing.

It is also not considered good form when shooting driven pheasants to fire at a low bird whatever danger there may be of it knocking your hat off. This is not so much an account of the element of danger but more because it is considered unsporting. Besides which you will look such a damned fool if you miss it.

Another annoyance which is particularly prevalent amongst foreigners, is the amount of shouting in which they are apt to indulge at the beginning of a drive. When the birds are being gently coaxed forward and being persuaded to get up in the air is not the time to enquire of a gun two pegs away of the state of his mother-in-law's health or what rate of exchange he got for his francs or dollars. Any sort of loud shouting is apt to send the birds scurrying back between the legs of the beaters.

The End of the Day

There are certain formalities to be observed at the end of the day of which the most important is the question for the guest of who to tip, and how much.

The answer to whom you tip is quite simple. You tip the head keeper and only the head keeper. Exactly how much is more difficult to lay down. The older generation in particular find it very hard to adjust to inflation and remember the day when a ten-bob note was considered a princely offering.

There are many who make it a rule to tip on a scale according to the success of the day, judged by the number of birds shot. This would seem to be fair enough. Certainly, ostentatious overtipping is something which is very much frowned upon but after a good day it is no time to be parsimonious. A basic minimum of a five pound note would seem to be about right nowadays and anything over ten pounds in the show-off class.

'YOURS'

One of the rituals at the end of the day is the laying out of the bag. This is the responsibility of the head keeper whilst the guns are discussing the last drive and having another go at the sloe gin and ginger wine. Then everyone gathers round as he walks down the line of dead birds, tapping each brace with his stick as he goes.

It is the custom for each guest gun to receive a brace of birds to take home with him – in the case of pheasants always a cock and a hen bird. The birds, tied together with a piece of twine by their necks, will be handed over by the head keeper who at the same time will offer to shake your hand. This is the time when the financial transaction takes place. You will already have the number of currency notes you have decided upon as a tip in the palm of your hand and take the opportunity of discreetly transferring them to him. He will then respectfully touch his hat to you – or not, as the case may be.

The final courtesy at the end of a shoot is that you should

be handed a game card. This consists of a specially printed card in the front of which there is a space for you to fill in the number of head shot under their various categories and, on the reverse side, a handwritten list of the names of your fellow guests, giving their correct rank and title. Thus you may learn for the first time that the fellow on the next peg who kept poaching all your birds and referred to only as Bimbo was in fact the Earl of Featherstonelaugh (pronounced Fanshawe) and much other information which can be immediately entered into your own game book upon your returning home, together with such comments as you may care to make in the space provided whilst the memory of the triumphs and disasters of the day are still fresh in your memory.

6

Living Dangerously

N ever, never, let your gun,
Pointed be at anyone,
All the pheasants ever bred
Will not repay for one man dead.

This is one of the best known and most quoted bits of dogma
around.

Fathers, and particularly those new to the game, quote it *ad
nauseum* to their children to impress upon them, not only the
advisability of not going around shooting people but also their
own worldy wisdom, learned in the hard school of experience.

It is, of course, utter tosh.

It ignores the fact that almost all gentlemen of an older
generation were trained early on in their lives, not only to
point a gun at anyone they were told to but make sure they
pressed the trigger as well. It is also to ignore that, although
we have now gone for rather longer than usual without a
world war, there are still so many perfectly bloody people
around it puts a rather less than fair value on the life of a
pheasant.

There is the example of one well-known gentleman of
ancient lineage who, becoming tired of his continuing exist-

ence, decided to end it. Accordingly he went through to the gun room and, pointing a gun at his own head, blew his brains out with a super magnum cartridge from the choke barrel of his favourite twelve-bore. Not before, however, being a tidy-minded chap, he had entered the date in the game book and, in the column marked 'various' recorded 'one baronet'.

None of which is to say that safety in the shooting field is not of paramount importance and should be drilled into the young from the very earliest age. Simple things like unloading before crossing a fence as well as between drives and keeping the safety catch on until you are about to fire when walking up, are normally things which are bred in the bone but this is not to say that every country-bred gentleman is, because of the way he has been brought up, a safe shot. Not by a very long chalk it isn't.

There must be few keepers on even the grandest of estates who do not bear the scars from wounds inflicted at one time or another by either his master or his guests and, by and large, these wounds are born uncomplainingly as one of the risks which go with the job.

Before the days of those shoots where you can rent a gun, it was unusual if all the guns were not personally known to each other as well as their performances in the field from earliest schooldays. Nor was there a head keeper worth his salt who did not know it all as well.

A good keeper after he had placed the guns for the first drive would then brief the beaters. 'Watch out on the left flank,' he might advise. 'That there Major Blastington-Smith is the end gun. If you find yourselves within range, you'll drop flat and stay there until the drive is over if you want to see your mother again,' and so on.

A gentleman's failings in this direction tend to be tolerated as a form of mild eccentricity and particularly if he happens to be the owner of some good shooting himself.

There is the true story of the proprietor of a particularly fine sporting estate where invitations to shoot were eagerly sought after. A fine shot in his day, unfortunately, with the passing of the years, he became increasingly blind so that it became more and more difficult for him to make out exactly what he was shooting at. His enthusiasm for the sport, however, did not diminish in proportion to the degree of his incapacity. When almost total blindness had descended he used to take a man-servant with him whose job it was to indicate to his master the general direction of any target which might present itself.

'Bird coming over right m'lord' he would cry and His Lordship would duly blast off with both barrels in the direction indicated.

For some time this arrangement worked admirably with very little damage to fur or feather but alas it is a story which has a sad ending. One day a friend, anxious for a return invitation to His Lordship's excellent shoot, rang up and invited him for a day on his own modest estate.

'Don't think I will,' he said. 'Getting dreadfully blind you know.'

'Good Heavens,' said his friend. 'Don't worry about that. Take your man with you like you always do.'

'Can't do that,' His Lordship explained. 'Shot him you know.'

And he had.

It should not be thought, however, that a certain tolerance towards the sort of minor accidents which inevitably occur from time to time in even the best organised shoots is extended to those occasions when more serious accidents occur.

There is just one unbreakable rule. In cases where the victim of a shooting accident requires urgent medical attention, necessitating the calling in of some outsider like the local doctor, *the person responsible for the accident shall never be named.* No matter how certainly the blame can be laid at one individual's door, an accident is never talked about afterwards. It is a rule that even the victim, if he survives the experience, respects.

I can remember some years ago being told by a keeper in the greatest confidence of an accident when one of the most renowned lady shots of her day was the victim of someone carelessly swinging across the line during a grouse drive. 'She dropped without a murmur,' he confided but I'll never know whether this was on account of the unwritten law of preserving a loyal silence or simply because she was too badly wounded to utter a protest.

This does not mean the perpetrator of an act of carelessness, which has serious repercussions, escapes without penalty. The man at whom the finger points must put up his gun and leave. Nor must he ever shoot again. That is the price of silence.

These high standards of gentlemanly behaviour, reminiscent of the finest traditions of honour being satisfied as existed in the heyday of duelling, would now appear to have become seriously eroded.

There was quite recently an incident when a retired Cabinet Minister, Lord Whitelaw, inadvertently and quite innocently peppered his host who happened to be occupying the next butt to him, during a grouse drive. Next morning this trivial affair was splashed across the headlines of the world press to the extent that I don't think the poor fellow will ever now live it down. This was the clearest breach of the rule of confidentiality, designed for the protection of minor offenders.

By contrast there was another recent occasion when the offender was an American visitor. It is perhaps unfortunate that he happened to be an American who as a race have earned a possibly undeserved reputation for undisciplined behaviour when out 'hunting', as they will insist on calling it.

The circumstances were that after the last pheasant drive of the day the guns were standing around engaged in sociable chit chat whilst the pickers-up were searching for the last of the dead or wounded and the bag was being laid out to be counted. Suddenly a cock pheasant which had been sitting tight, unwisely decided that the time had come when he could safely take his departure. He reckoned, however, without one of the guns in the American party who had neglected to observe the most cardinal rule of unloading his gun when the drive was over, and who immediately let fly with both barrels. The pheasant escaped unscathed but a group of beaters nearby who had fallen out for a smoke came into the direct line of fire. The combined fire power of two barrels wounded no less than six of them, two grievously.

As the American in question was of no special social or political distinction it was not something which warranted a great deal of press coverage except possibly as an entry in the Guinness Book of Records. However, it was a serious transgression against the code of behaviour as it applied to serious accidents when shooting. Far from retiring even for a short time from the field of conflict, he turned up punctually for the first drive of the day on the following morning. By the standards which prevail today it is not easy to find fault with what not so long ago would have been regarded as a flagrant breech of etiquette. After all the chap had probably paid for his day's sport in advance.

As a footnote for those whose earnest desire it is to identify themselves as belonging to the old school rather than with the more newly arrived, here is a useful hint which may help with the camouflage.

When referring to the accidents which occur almost inevitably when out shooting, it should be noted that any gentleman who happens to be at the receiving end will never refer to himself as having been 'wounded'. It is one of the traditions reaching back to long before the Battle of Waterloo that only other ranks are ever wounded. Officers and gentleman are 'hit', which is quite a different matter. To be hit is the opposite of being missed and that is all part of what is after all just a game which you can go on playing. It is only members of the lower social orders who take things so seriously as to allow themselves to become wounded and have to drop out.

It should also be noted that there are certain targets which, assuming that you miss whatever you were aiming at in the first place, it is less done to hit than others.

At the very top of the list comes one's host which may have been the cause of the incident involving the ex-Cabinet Minister quoted earlier being taken more seriously than it need have been. By the same token, the fact that the American gentleman only wounded a few beaters who come further down the list of what constitutes fair game might have seemed somehow to have lessened his guilt.

Perhaps it might be helpful here to list the various people you should not hit or wound in order of importance.

They are:

Your host.
Your host's dog.
Any of your fellow guns, including the spotty youth with the runny nose.
Any of your fellow guests' dogs.
The Head Keeper.
All under-keepers.
All beaters and especially the older slower-moving ones.
Any women or children who happen to be standing around.
The man leaning on his bicycle at the corner of the lane.

The most dangerous time, particularly for the beaters advancing towards eight fully armed gentlemen of various degrees of excitability, is when they start to get within range, which generally coincides with the time when the number of birds deciding to take to the wing is at its highest. To minimise the risk it is the usual practice for the head keeper or other responsible person amongst the advancing forces to blow loudly on a horn or a similar instrument. This is the signal for the guns to stop firing forward at approaching birds and turn round and only continue to fire at birds which have passed over their heads.

I can remember on a recent occasion when an inexperienced gun got so carried away as to ignore the warning and shooting at a low-flying bird duly wounded one of the beaters. That the one he hit happened to be the one who was blowing the horn was generally regarded by one and all as making it a very serious breach of protocol indeed.

That there should be considered to be some sort of social gap between those who are standing and those who are beating is natural enough. Although it is by no means always the case, it was something which greatly worried the titled owner of a large estate in Northumberland which he inherited from his father before the last war. His particular eccentricity was that he was not only a man of great learning but held political views of the extreme left. His espousal of the Communist cause, however, did nothing to inhibit his inherited love of traditional field sports and especially shooting. After inheriting he continued to give very grand shooting parties but managed to reconcile the seeming contradiction of the privileges inherent in being one of the 'haves' as against the 'have-nots' in a most ingenious fashion.

On big driving days he had his beaters fully armed as well as his guests and, at the beginning of each drive, the two lines advanced against each other firing as they went.

It is recorded that it was his guests' courage which broke before the nerves of the beaters who, when it came to the final confrontation, found the 'haves' cowering behind trees or dug into holes in the ground.

7

Shooting Talk

Gentlemen who shoot have, like any other group of people with an interest in common, a language or a way of expressing themselves which is their own. This is not a deliberate piece of one-upmanship to prove something or establish themselves to be not as other men are. It is not nearly so tiresome an affectation as that adopted by, say, people who sail boats who will insist on calling a rope a sheet and make landlubbers scratch their heads before deciding which way is port and which starboard. None the less it is just as well for the newcomer to the game to get things right.

Gunmanship

There could hardly be a less technical piece of technology than a sporting gun. In these days of computerisation which has produced a new language of its own and which is completely incomprehensible to the outsider, a gun remains quite simply a gun. If, however, somebody refers to their gun as 'my twelve-bore', it is useful to know that this refers to the gauge of the barrels and, in consequence, the power of the gun. The twelve-bore is generally accepted as the standard size for a gun for the average adult male but they can go down in size to a four-bore

...YAK, YAK, YAK...

or even a two-bore which are virtually small cannon, although still fired from the shoulder. It should be noted that the smaller the number, the larger the gauge and the larger the amount of shot it can carry. A four-bore used to be not uncommon for use by wildfowlers. When it was discharged into a flock of ducks the spread of shot was calculated to create carnage.

At the other end of the scale there are sixteen-bore, twenty-bore and twenty-four bore guns, the latter being a very light gun considered suitable for ladies. Boys who are introduced to shooting at an early age often start off with a twenty- or sixteen-bore and are sometimes so proficient with them that they continue to shoot with them when adult. The most popular gun of all to start a boy with is a .410 (a four-ten). This is a very light gun indeed and sometimes made so that the barrel can fold back alongside the stock and so can easily and inconspicuously be carried down the trouser leg. For this reason it is sometimes known as the 'poacher's gun'.

Then there is the matter of the choke. This refers to the narrowing of the gun barrel towards the muzzle which has the effect of both narrowing the pattern of the shot and causing it to carry for a greater distance. It is common to have a greater choke on the left-hand barrel of a double-barrelled shot-gun on the principle that the target will in all probability be further away by the time the second barrel is fired. Because of the grouping of the shot, a shot with the choke barrel is much more likely to prove lethal than with a wider spread of pellets. The writer can well remember when as a small boy he was allowed to stand behind the host at a grown-ups' pheasant shoot. The host was an elderly Admiral who, quite apart from being, like Lord Nelson, blind in one eye, was an incredibly bad shot. It happened that at the end of one drive during which the Admiral had missed absolutely everything, there was a sudden crashing in the bushes. The Admiral, raising his gun, fired in the general direction of what he thought to be a startled roe deer. 'Got him with the choke barrel,' he roared triumphantly; only it was not a roe deer but a beater who, when he realised he had come out opposite where the Admiral was standing and knowing his reputation as a dangerous shot, decided to make a dive for safety over a low dyke. The Admiral proved too quick for him and caught him in the back of the neck at around fifty paces.

A Right and Left

To 'get a Right and Left' means getting a hit with each barrel. Usually this means killing two birds with consecutive shots out of, say, a covey of partridges. There are, however, many examples of right and lefts of a much more remarkable nature. My own favourite is of an acquaintance who was walking in line through a field of turnips when a pheasant got up in front of him. He was carrying his gun under his arm and, in his haste to raise it, one trigger caught in a button of his jacket, discharging the right barrel which shot through the toe of his boot. Then with his left barrel he killed the pheasant before hobbling off the field of battle.

It is interesting to conjecture with the introduction of the sort of gun which has the barrels one on top of the other instead of being more conventionally placed side by side how the feat of getting a Right and Left should be described. Somehow a Top and Bottom doesn't sound quite right.

Birds of a Feather

One of the oddest quirks in shoot-speak is the difficulty which seems to arise whenever game of any sort is referred to in the plural. Many game birds, of course, are never described in the plural: grouse, for example, or snipe or woodcock. Duck in all their varieties like mallard, wigeon, teal and so on, do not have a plural description. On the other hand, the goose does, being referred to collectively as geese, although one of the commonest of the species, the greylag, has no plural whilst the almost equally common pinkfoot can be described when there are more than one of them as pinkfeet.

The real difficulty comes, however, when referring to part-ridges and pheasants. It is perfectly correct to go pheasant or partridge shooting but incorrect to shoot pheasant or partridge. What you shoot are pheasants or partridges.

It is all rather the same as calling the room set aside in many large houses for the playing of a game called billiards as the billiard room although nobody has ever been known to play a game called billiard in it or on anything other than a billiards table. Just as nobody would claim to wish to indulge in a game of billiard so nobody would correctly say they were going out to shoot pheasant when what they are doing is going pheasant shooting. This confuses a lot of people including foreigners.

Another thing worth remembering is that when game birds become dead they are counted by the brace. Thus five living pheasants would become two and a half brace when dead. Everything else like duck or ground game are counted in pairs.

Whilst they are alive both partridges and grouse stay together as families after they have learned to fly and are known as coveys. Later in the season coveys of grouse tend to join up together and are then known as packs. Pheasants never form coveys or packs.

Flocks of wild geese are known as 'gaggles' but only when they are on the ground. When flying together they are known as 'skeins'. A number of duck in the air together are known as a 'flight' and a few snipe together are described as a 'wisp'. Pigeons go about in flocks as do many other species of bird who do not come into the game bird category. The exception is a flock of starlings which is known as a 'murmuration' – an inapt description if ever there was one.

Ifs and Butts

When shooting driven grouse the guns are concealed in hides made out of piles of stones or turfs of peat. These are called 'butts'. This is only, however, when shooting grouse. Any other form of concealment for shooting anything else is a 'hide'. The object of using a hide is to get whatever is being shot at to approach as close as possible before becoming a target. The exception to this is shooting pheasants where the guns are placed at 'stands' or 'pegs' which are in the open. These are usually placed at the bottom of a valley or dip in the ground so that the birds when they come over are as high up in the air as possible so making them more difficult to kill, which was the object of driving them over the guns in the first place.

Hit or Miss

In the event of your hitting a bird which does not immediately become manifestly dead, it becomes a matter of loudly expressed speculation by any witnesses present as to how slightly or seriously the bird in question has been damaged. It can be a 'leg down' situation which means that as it will require both legs to enable it to get up again when it lands it will be unable to do so and thus become more easily 'picked'. On the other hand it can be adjudged a 'runner' which means, particularly in the case of pheasants and partridges, that they can take off like Olympic sprinters the moment they hit the ground and lead the best of dogs a merry dance. The opinion voiced by the onlookers as to whether a bird which is down is a runner or not is usually as reliable as that of the average race-course tipster.

Other hits are often dismissed as merely 'disturbing a feather or two' by the know-all spectators with no lasting disadvantage to the bird. On the day following a shoot a good keeper will usually pick up quite a number of dead birds which have only had a feather or two disturbed.

In fact it is quite possible to kill a bird stone dead and for it to carry on flying for a considerable distance before it finally drops. This is called a 'towering' bird because a bird so hit (usually in the head) will often tower up almost vertically to quite a height before it finally drops.

Gun-Speak

Conversation between guns when out shooting is conducted almost entirely in monosyllables. 'Mark!', 'Damn!', 'Over!', 'Shot!', 'Blast!' and so on are common cries by shooting men in various degrees of excitement or exasperation.

Dog-Speak

Spoken communication between dog and master or mistress in only slightly more elaborate than communication between fellow guns. 'Go seek!' 'Hi lorst! Hi lorst! Hi lorst!', 'Heel, heah!' or 'Come back here you bloody idiot or I'll kick your arse so hard a pigeon will fly out!' are some of the commoner conversational gambits.

Although there are owners of dogs who are prone to bedecking themselves with whistles of all types and sizes, this is not always a very practical idea as it is apt to sound like Crewe Railway Station in the rush hour when they all start whistling away.

It is also usual for canine companions of the field to be given short, abrupt names like Snipe, Jet, Rock or Sam. This is because names like Goldilocks Sweetheart of Bryuncepeth Magna do not roll so readily off the tongue in moments of stress.

8

Sporting Records

A s has been remarked somewhere else in this small book, it was the wealthy Victorians who first conceived a passion for proving that they could do everything better and on a bigger scale than the next man. In no aspect of their leisured lives was this more apparent than when it came to shooting.

The rivalries between owners of the great estates who vied with each other to produce ever bigger bags was intense. This was particularly true of the big estates of Norfolk and Suffolk which were laid out entirely for sport and the 'score' after any of the big battues, and particularly those at which Royalty had been present, made known up and down the country within hours of the last shot being fired.

The expense involved was enormous. Lord Walsingham spent almost the entire family fortune in giving shooting parties for the Prince of Wales. The first part of the family inheritance to be sacrificed as surplus to requirements was his princely town house which occupied the site overlooking Green Park on which the Ritz Hotel now stands. One year he actually moved out of his family seat, Merton Hall, and retired to the South of France to give the Prince a free rein. The Prince moved in with all his retinue and when, after the the season was over,

Walsingham returned, it was to find that his once famous cellar of the finest wines had been drunk entirely dry.

The tradition set by Edward VII for holding absurdly extravagant shooting parties was continued by his son, the much more staid and strait-laced King George V who was reckoned to be amongst the very finest shots in the Kingdom. Later in his life, however, there is evidence that he had become sated. His son, who reigned briefly as Edward VIII, recounted the story of an occasion when driving back with his father from a record-breaking shoot. For a long time the King sat silent in their carriage, staring out of the window. Then he roused himself to remark, 'I think perhaps we overdid it today.' Although most of the male members of the Royal Family today are keen shots (the Queen is an enthusiastic picker-up), Edward VIII never really got the bug. He preferred the bright lights of London and his suburban private residence, Fort Belvedere, where there was no shooting and where he could spend much of his time courting Mrs Simpson. Sandringham, which Queen Victoria's German husband, Prince Albert, urged on her that she should buy for their eldest son on the grounds that no English gentleman should be without his own sporting estate, never appealed to Edward VIII who, on his abdication, sold it to his brother, George VI, who described it as 'dear old Sandringham, the place I love most in all the world'. It has been the Royal Family's favourite retreat ever since, when not able to get up to their even-more-sporting Scottish estate at Balmoral.

One of the more remarkable (and more vulgar) sporting records ever achieved in the heyday of the Victorian grandees was that achieved by Lord Walsingham himself on his grouse moor, Blubberhouse, which happens to be not in Scotland but in Lancashire. One of his more competitive cronies remarked that, as it promised to be a poor season and Blubberhouse was, in any event, a fairly no-account sort of moor, it would not be worthwhile shooting over it. Walsingham boasted that he could shoot over a thousand grouse to his own gun in one day and proceeded to prove it.

Blubberhouse is not a big moor but it is an extremely oddly-shaped one. It consists of two large expanses of heather, joined by a narrow neck, rather after the fashion of an egg timer. It becomes so narrow at the neck that it can be covered by a single gun and it was here that Walsingham took up his position. Thus the grouse which have a marked preference for flying over their own familiar heather, tended, when driven from one half of the moor to another, to converge over His Lordship's head.

His simple plan was to have one set of beaters drive the birds over him from one direction and then, turning round in his butt, have another set of beaters immediately drive them back again from the opposite direction. And so it continued all through the day, with Tommy Walsingham blazing away merrily, scarcely having to move a foot whilst the beaters harried the birds back and forth. It is said that he hardly missed a shot and the confirmed total for the day was 1,070 grouse.

How many of these actually fell to his gun is unknown because so exhausted did the birds eventually become that the beaters were picking them up unable to fly any further and the number which had thus surrendered were added to the total. Moreover, the large number of birds destroyed so depleted stocks that Blubberhouse was ruined as a moor for many years afterwards.

Incidentally, the largest number of grouse shot in one day by a single gun walking up is 440. This feat was achieved by the overweight Maharajah Duleep Singh on the Grandtully Castle moor in Perthshire, which he rented for a number of years, in 1871. Duleep, The Black Prince as he was known, was an altogether remarkable figure in sporting circles at the end of the century. Deprived of his vast estates and palaces in India by the British whilst still a youth, he devoted the rest of his life, with only one minor show of revolt, to establishing himself as an English country gentleman. He bought estates at Elveden in Suffolk which he built up into being one of the finest sporting estates in the country. Because of his great weight he had to have specially constructed shooting sticks on which to perch between drives which makes his achievement walking over the Grandtully moors all the more remarkable.

One of the Maharajah's grumbles was that, when his estates were taken over by the East India Company, they also pinched one of his family's most prized possessions, the Koh-I-Noor diamond, then the largest diamond in the world.

The Company then proceeded to present the diamond to Queen Victoria who, as Empress of India, had it set in her crown and refused, despite all appeals and notwithstanding invitations to her son to shoot at Elveden, to give it back. From then on Duleep always referred to Her Majesty as Mrs Fagin, after Dickens's thief in *Oliver Twist*. Not at all a sporting old bird.

In a fit of pique, Duleep surrendered his lavish pension from the British Government and set out in a boat for India in an attempt to regain his lost possessions. He was stopped on the way and eventually returned to England and Elveden, was given his pension back and resigned himself to spending the rest of his days enjoying the life of a sporting squire. When he died the estate was sold to the First Lord Iveagh, the head of the Guinness family and one of the first of the 'new money' aristocracy – collectively known as 'The Beerage' on account of the large number who had made their fortunes from breweries – who were busy buying up the estates of the old landed families who had dissipated their fortunes.

Today there are not many, even amongst the richest of landowners, who can afford to run their estates on the scale of those days when they sought to achieve glory through the number of birds they could drive over the guns. It was an ostentation which cost them dear and much of it must be laid at the door of Edward VII who dearly loved ostentation and the company of the very rich whether self-made or not.

Even he almost went too far when, against all advice, he accepted the invitation of Baron Hirsch, the head of an immensely wealthy Hungarian family, who had made the family fortune from money-lending, to shoot over his vast estates where the size of the bags was reported as being astronomical. The reports proved to be no exaggeration and far larger than anything which could ever be dreamed of in England which only had the effect of making the Royal visit all the more deplorable in the eyes of the older English aristocracy.

In recent years there has been only one serious and successful attempt to establish a new game record. This was by a Lincolnshire potato farmer, Joe (now Sir Joseph) Nickerson, whose other claim to fame is that he was the host who was recently so publicly peppered with shot during a grouse drive on his Yorkshire moors by ex-Cabinet Minister, Lord Whitelaw.

The total number of partridges shot in 1952 by five guns in one day was 2,015. This amazing total was achieved by hand-picked, expert shots, each with a loader and picker-up/spotter, being rushed from stand to stand in Land Rovers over the flat Lincolnshire land and with no time for such social niceties as a protracted lunch break and society chit-chat. The previous best was 1,671 in 1905 by Lord Leicester on his nearby Holkham estate in Norfolk. I think most people today, given the choice, would have preferred to have been shooting with Lord Leicester.

Here is a list of some of the more important big bags achieved over the last hundred years or so:

PHEASANTS

Where	When	Host	Total
Sandringham (Norfolk)	4th Nov. 1896	Prince of Wales	3,114

Water Priory (Yorks)	5th Dec. 1909	Lord Nunburnholme	3,824
Hall Barn (Bucks)	18th Dec. 1913	Lord Burnham	3,937

... all dwarfed by the Hungarians where the record bag made on 10th December 1909 by Count Karolyi on his Tot Magyar estates was 6,125 pheasants.

PARTRIDGES

Where	*When*	*Host*	*Total*
The Grange (Hants)	4th Nov. 1897	Lord Ashburton	1,461
Sandringham (Norfolk)	10th Nov. 1905	Prince of Wales	1,342
Holkham (Norfolk)	7th Dec. 1905	Lord Leicester	1,671

... but even Mr Nickerson's new record in Lincolnshire in 1952 of 2,015 was overtopped, again by the Hungarians when Baron Horsch in 1892 on his St Johann estates shot 2,870.

GROUSE

Where	*When*	*Host*	*Total*
Roan Fell (Scottish Borders)	30th Aug. 1911	Duke of Buccleuch	2,523
Broomhead (Yorks)	27th Aug. 1913	Mr Rimington-Wilson	2,843
Littledale (Lancs)	12th Aug. 1915	Lord Sefton	2,929

HARES

Holkham (Norfolk)	19th Dec. 1977	Lord Leicester	1,215

RABBITS

Blenheim Palace (Oxon)	7th Oct. 1898	Duke of Marlborough	6,943

The record for a single gun shooting driven grouse is Lord Walsingham's unique performance already mentioned at Blubberhouse when he shot 1,070. Maharajah Duleep Singh, who had a record of 440 grouse in one day walking up over dogs, excelled himself on his Elveden estate when on the 8th September 1876 he killed 780 partridges to his own gun. One of the finest feats ever achieved was when on the famous Wemmergill moor in Yorkshire Sir Fredrick Milbank of Barningham (another famous Yorkshire moor) killed 190 grouse to his own gun in *one single drive*. This was only excelled when Lord de Grey (later Marquess of Ripon) shot 240 partridges in a single drive – but that again was in Hungary which, in the opinion of the true-blue Englishman, does not really count.

9

Shooting and the Law

O n the first of September, one Sunday morn
I shot a hen pheasant in standing corn;
Without a licence, contrive who can,
A greater collection of crimes, against God and Man.

This little rune describes very well the balance which, traditionally, has always existed between the obligations respected
by a sporting gentleman to his neighbours, the Good Lord and
the Law in, roughly speaking, that order.

It would be quite unthinkable that he should, for example,
transgress by shooting a pheasant on the opening day of the
partridge season – the pheasant season not opening until the
1st October – and that he should add to the gravity of this
offence by doing so on a Sunday morning when by rights he
should have been reading the lesson in church.

Although on the Continent Sunday mornings are made
hideous by the rattle of musketry as the local population let off
at everything from larks to nightingales, Sunday has always
been respected in England as a day of rest for quarry and hunter
alike. No matter if the most important day in the sporting
calendar, the opening of the grouse shooting on the 12th August,
should fall on a Sunday. The Lord's Day takes priority.

'OUT OF SEASON'

It should hardly be necessary to point out that it is a matter of *noblesse oblige* that a hen pheasant out of season should be more sacrosanct than a cock but it might be necessary to make an observation about the standing corn. In these days of much improved agricultural methods there is nowadays very little standing corn on the 1st September anyway but this indicates the respect in which the landlord has always held his obligations to his tenants. To go trampling after a covey of partridges which has sought refuge in a field where the crop has not yet been harvested would be considered to be a gross breach of good manners. It would come in much the same category as the local hunt riding over a farmer's crop of spring wheat.

The reference to not holding a licence shows a reasonable respect for the law of the land which requires everyone who owns a gun to take out a licence. The sort of licence varies with the type of weapon. An ordinary sporting gun, for example, only requires a gun licence which currently costs £12.00 from the local police station, to be renewed after three years for a fee of £8.00. There was a time when a shot-gun licence cost five shillings and was all that was required by a farmer who only used his gun to shoot rabbits or keep down vermin. A nob who intended to use his gun to shoot game also required a game licence which was a much more expensive business requiring, in pre-war days, the expenditure of the considerable sum of five pounds.

Should one want to license a rifle more high-powered than an air-gun, it is necessary when applying for the licence for the owner to produce written evidence of either permission to use the weapon where there is little danger to human life, as when deer stalking, or of belonging to a rifle or pistol club where the weapon is only used for target shooting under controlled conditions.

When quite recently some maniac went berserk with a lethal weapon in the streets of a quiet township in the Home Counties, shooting several innocent citizens before shooting himself, there was a great public outcry, initiated by the usual lunatic fringe, demanding the immediate banning of any sort of gun licensed in any form or at best for the many thousands of people who owned ordinary sporting guns to be required to keep them under lock and key at a police station. This has, however, led to a complete ban on certain weapons, including sawn-off shot-guns, rocket launchers (except for fireworks) and trench mortars.

Although the Home Secretary, Mr Douglas Hurd, appeared to wither slightly under the fury of the onslaught, under new legislation the keeping of a licensed sporting gun in one's own home has not yet become a capital offence – nor has there been any marked increase in the number of shot-gun owners spraying the lads of the village with pellets from their twelve-bores after a Saturday night out in the local. The selling and the custody of other more warlike automatic weapons in their various forms is, of course, quite a different matter.

Other laws and regulations as they relate to field sports are more straightforward or more obscure according to the way you look at them.

Take, for example, the laws relating to trespass and rights of way.

The right of the domestic farm duck when crossing a public highway is perhaps a byway of the law which is not widely understood by the public. The law is that, should a family of ducks choose to go for a swim on a pond on the opposite side of a public highway to their normal place of residence, they do so at their own risk. When, however, they decide to return, they have the legal right of way. Thus any motorist so incautious as to plough into a line of Aylesburys waddling their way homewards, does so at the peril of having to pay the owner of the ducks adequate compensation for their loss.

This is rather the opposite of the case when a burglar is

seeking to invade your home. If it is evident that, in committing this act of trespass, it is also his intention to cause the householder bodily harm, he is entitled to repel him by whatever means he can, including the use of a properly licensed firearm and providing he gives due warning to the intruder of his intention to do so. Should, however, the burglar, loaded down with the family silver, be in the act of making his escape, to try to prevent him with a well-aimed shot in his bum, is a serious offence against his person and a denial of his civil rights.

There are other strange anomalies with regard to shot-guns, as opposed to rifles. One is that it is possible to buy a shot-gun without the necessity of producing a licence but it is illegal to try to sell one without a licence currently in force, as many a defenceless widow has discovered to her cost when innocently trying to dispose of her late husband's gun to an unscrupulous gun dealer.

The trick is to induce the seller to leave the gun on pretext of having it valued and then to refuse to surrender it unless a current licence is produced. In doing this they have the full backing of the law.

The law of trespass has a great number of anomalies and to understand it is not made any easier in that, as in many other instances, the law is different in Scotland from England. Poaching which is to be found on private land for the purpose of taking game is only an aggravated form of trespass, the degree of aggravation being in direct relationship with whether poached game is found in the possession of the trespasser or not. Trespass can be a serious or trivial matter according to the amount of damage done by the trespasser. To take game illegally is a serious matter but not nearly so serious as it was in the last century.

Until the Industrial Revolution altered the face of Britain in the middle of the nineteenth century, all the power was in the hands of the great landowning families. Not to own land was to be nothing and no one. The great landowners monopolised not only the House of Lords but the House of Commons as well where, apart from a smattering of lawyers and bankers, almost all the members sat in the landowning interest.

One of the privileges most jealously guarded by the landowners was their exclusive right to take game. No one below the social rank of Esquire was allowed to shoot game and the buying and selling of game was illegal. Even today to deal in game requires a game dealer's licence.

To be caught poaching so much as a rabbit was punishable by imprisonment or transportation. An armed poacher caught in possession of a hare on the Broadlands estate of the Prime Minister of the day Lord Melbourne, was hanged in public from the walls of Winchester jail, despite a plea for clemency to the Prime Minister himself.

'Unless we enforce the strictest laws to protect private property the whole Constitution will collapse,' he declared.

By the turn of the century there were more people in prison for poaching offences than for all other offences put together. They crowded out the prison hulks moored in the Thames and Australia in particular was colonised almost entirely with convicted poachers.

To demonstrate just how seriously the law has been eroded from the landowners' point of view since so not so far off days (they were still hanging poachers up to the turn of the century), it is only necessary to cite the recent case of the highly respected Yorkshire landowner and keen shooting man, Lord Mountgarret.

His Lordship and a party of friends were enjoying a day grouse shooting on his Yorkshire moors when, in the middle of a drive, a very large hot-air balloon appeared from nowhere, coming lower and lower until it was literally hovering between the line of beaters and the guns, to the very serious detriment of the day's sport.

Whether the passengers in the basket suspended beneath the balloon were waving their hankies and generally trying to join in the fun or whether their intentions were of a less amiable nature is not entirely clear. Either way, Lord Mountgarret was not in the least amused and, raising his twelve-bore, let fly. As he has the reputation of being a remarkably fine shot and not the sort of person to score a complete miss at a target rather larger than a fair-sized haystack closely above his head, it is safe to absolve his Lordship of any wish to inflict grievous bodily harm and to do other than express his gravest displeasure at this trespass in what was undoubtedly his airspace.

So affronted were the balloonists, however, and so blind to the gravity of their offence that they called in the police. It was Lord Mountgarret who was hauled up before the magistrates and who narrowly escaped transportation. Instead he was fined and had his shot-guns removed. *O tempora! O mores!* In earlier times he could have had the ringleader hanged from the clock above the pavilion of the Yorkshire Cricket Ground at Headingley where he is Chairman of the Club.

Another aspect of laws governing trespass and rights of way which is currently exciting the anti-landowner lobby and particularly their anti-bloodsports fanatical supporters, centres round what they claim should be the complete right of public access to all those areas extending to many hundreds of thousands of acres which are designated common land.

In fact, before the privatisation of land by the Acts of Enclosure, practically the whole of England was common land, but this did not mean that it was land over which no rights existed. All land has always been the subject of a bundle of different rights, like mineral rights, grazing rights, sporting rights and so on, and these rights by no means always belong to the same person. Rights of way and areas to which the public has a right of access are specifically designated as such. Nor need public right of access mean an unrestricted right. Even access to public parks may be restricted to within certain hours and subject to by-laws like keeping dogs on leads or not walking on the grass. The only land over which the public are allowed to shoot (providing they hold a gun licence) is on the shore between the high and low water tide-marks, which belongs to the Queen as does the sea bed round Britain including the whole of the North Sea shelf. The free sporting rights on the foreshore are by Royal permission except in the Shetland and Orkney Isles which are governed by Udal rather than Feudal Law, under which all foreshore rights, including the rights to the seaweed on which some islanders graze their sheep, belong to the individual farmers. Which just goes to show that when it comes to a matter of trespass nothing is quite what it seems to be. Not by a long chalk.

Many of the best grouse moors in the north of England are on common land and on which the sporting rights are strictly preserved for the landowners, just as, in most cases, the grazing rights are strictly preserved for those farmers who have an established claim. The public are excluded from many other areas of common land for a variety of reasons like the preservation of wildlife such as rare plants or the nesting habitat of rare species of birds.

Without the protection of game afforded by the law, all game would be virtually extinct in this country, as the French discovered following the Revolution and as have the Americans who will issue a licence for anyone to shoot anything, including each other, more or less anywhere.

The legal restrictions on the selling of game may seem to be an archaic survival of the bad old days. That this is not the case is shown by the case of the wild goose. Wild geese have never enjoyed any sort of protection by the law and could therefore be freely offered for sale without proof that they had been legally come by. So vigorously were they persecuted after the war that the migrating flocks of geese which had formerly reached plague proportions to the extent of the ruination of farmers' crops on which they descended, started to become scarce. On the intervention of the great lobbyist for the protection of birds, Sir Peter Scott, a law was introduced some ten years ago banning the sale of geese, with the result that they have again multiplied and there are many farmers around who now stick pins into the effigy of the well-meaning Sir Peter.

By another strange quirk in the law, whilst it is a great offence to poach a salmon from a privately owned stretch of river or net them illegally in the sea, the moment the fish is removed from the scene of the crime, it can be freely offered for sale to a fishmonger or anyone else. To impose a similar ban to the one on the selling of game would seem to be a simple enough solution to the scandalous escalation of salmon poaching by ruthless gangs of criminals.

The crime of poaching and its association with trespass has undergone many vicissitudes of change since the days when an out-of-work farm labourer was hanged for taking a hare which rightly belonged to the Prime Minister of England. There are now some who feel that it is the 'haves' who are, in general, the greater in need of the protection of the law from the 'have-nots', but that is something which is outside the scope of this work.

For those who, at least, do not wish to offend against the birds themselves, the dates between which they can be legally killed is given here:

The red grouse may be legally shot between the 12th August and the 10th December. Note, however, that Black Game which share the grouse's moorland habitat may not, like the capercailzie, be killed until the 20th August, or the ptarmigan which lives on the very tops of the mountains until the 1st September if you can climb up that far.

The partridge season opens on the 1st September and goes

on until the 1st February. Pheasant shooting officially starts a month later on the 1st October. Wild duck from August to March. Woodcock, September to the 1st February. Snipe, October to the 1st February. Hares can be officially shot between the 1st August and the last day of February but rabbits can be shot all the year round and so can woodpigeons.

'THE OLD COCK'

10

The Shooting Party Hostess

*I*n the more spacious days of the Edwardians to be invited
to shoot usually involved being invited to join a house party
lasting several days – and, almost more importantly, nights.

House parties given to shoot or to hunt or to be involved in
any sort of activity which necessitated leaving town were as
much hedged around with convention as any other form of
socialising which was the full-time preoccupation of gentlemen
and, to an even greater extent, gentlemen's wives. The house
party also had tricky problems of protocol which were pecu-
liarly its own. Chief amongst these were the sleeping arrangements of the guests.

Practically all Edward VII's *affaires de la main gauche* were
conducted, or at least started, during shooting parties in English
country houses; but they conformed to the same rules of social
behaviour as applied to everyone else. That is to say, it would
be unthinkable that, as so often appears to happen today,
couples who were unmarried should on arrival be conducted
to the same bedroom, however widely known and accepted
their liaison might be. Further, it was never the lady on whom
the initiative fell of joining the gentleman in his bedroom after
lights out. It was the gentleman who was demanded by protocol
to seek out the lady. Thus it was that even those of the Blood

Royal were expected to join the general traffic of gentlemen tiptoeing along the corridors of stately homes, bumping into one another and cursing under their breath as they sought the correct door handle to turn.

Nor should the activities of the previous night be allowed to interfere to the slightest degree with the arrangements for the following day's sport. No matter how late hours had been kept in the billiards room or at the card table nor how sleepless those in the bedroom, a punctual appearance, properly break-fasted and turned out, was *de rigueur* at the exact time stated for the move off. To be late was only excusable by death.

It says much for the stamina of those Edwardians that the breakfasts they consumed were gargantuan and not in-frequently assisted by more than a few hairs from the tail of the dog which had bitten them during the night before. 'Shoot-ing powder', it used to be called, or 'jumping powder' in the case of hunting men. Then, of course, many of them did die quite young.

Times have altered from those days. Shooting parties now frequently put up at hotels with or without extra-marital attachments and the traditions of excessive consumption of food and drink are now less strictly observed. This relieves the shooting party hostess of many of her former responsibilities; none the less there are still occasions when houses or shooting lodges are taken by shooting or stalking parties and the demands of hospitality beyond simply the provision of hot baths and clean linen are called for.

The most important of these extends no further than the kitchen. Nothing establishes the reputation of a hostess who desires to be thought highly of than an authoritative knowledge of the preparation and the serving of game. Thus it may be that the notes which follow, limited though they are to purely culinary matters, will prove to be helpful.

★ ★ ★

The Hanging of Game

There is much nonsense talked on the subject of how long game should be hung.

All game birds are at their best eaten on the day they are shot. There is no advantage in allowing *rigor mortis* to set in and then allowing a further indeterminate period for the muscles to relax, which is all that hanging does. If the birds are not eaten soon after they are shot, however, this is necessary, otherwise they will be tough. How long a bird should be hung for depends entirely on the conditions under which they are kept.

There is also the factor that some people claim to prefer their game 'high' which means in a more advanced stage of decomposition. The taste for rotten or 'high' game is an acquired one and much affected by an older generation. A test of whether a pheasant was sufficiently high to be fit for the table was to hang it up by the tail until the maggots had done their work sufficiently for it to fall to the floor.

The correct way to hang any bird is on a hook through the lower beak and under conditions which are as cool as possible with plenty of air. Most important of all is that the room in which they are hung should be fly-, and particularly, blue-bottle-proof. Bluebottles do the most damage, laying their eggs which hatch out as maggots and particularly in any bird which has been badly shot.

Under perfect conditions birds will keep for a very considerable time. The fifth Earl of Lonsdale – the 'Yellow Earl' – was in the custom of presenting the senior partner of the family lawyers with a brace of grouse on his birthday which fell towards the end of March. The grouse shooting ends on the 10th December and the birds were always in perfect condition.

That was in the days before refrigeration but when every large household in the country had an outside walk-in game larder the walls of which were of zinc gauze so that the wind could blow through the pin-sized holes, too small to let in flies. In warm weather any servant entering the larder to fetch game had orders, under penalty of instant dismissal, to close the door immediately behind them lest a single fly gained admittance.

It was also always customary when sending gifts of game to friends to note, in the space provided on the game box, the date on which the birds had been shot and, out of consideration for a recipient who might be so unfortunate as not to have an outside game larder, to send them ready for the table.

Today when 'high' birds are not in so great a demand a few days hanging in the back kitchen should suit most tastes. If kept longer in warm conditions to get the 'gamey' flavour, do not let it worry you over much if they collect a few maggots. Just scrape them off before cooking. Incidentally, live maggots make very good bait for fishing. They can be kept almost indefinitely in dry meal.

The Age of the Bird

The age of the bird is not as important when it comes to cooking, as it is between an old boiling fowl and a young chicken but young birds are of course much better. If you are given the birds you have no option but to make the best of it but if you are buying them from the game dealer you do.

It is much easier to tell a young animal, like a rabbit, from an old one by just looking at it – to make matters easier a young rabbit's ears tear much more easily than an old one.

In the case of birds like a pheasant, partridge, or, less easily, a grouse, their legs are the easiest guide. An old bird's legs will be grey and horny with, in the case of pheasant cock birds, much bigger, tougher spurs. A young bird's legs are much more yellow (except French partridges which are much more red). More sure identification is in the wing feathers, the smaller ones, particularly in the case of partridges, are rather more sharply pointed. When buying birds it should be only necessary for you to let the game dealer see you looking at wing feathers or inspecting the bird's anus for him to take you for an expert and not try any tricks. There is no need really to know what you are looking for.

The Cooking

When it comes to cooking game birds, there is no particular mystique about it or any specially acquired expertise which cannot be mastered by anyone and without the need to take a cordon bleu cookery course. It is, however, possible to excite the envy of your less talented friends and gain a reputation for knowing your way about a game larder by observing a few simple rules.

It is, for example, one of the more profound truths that the smaller the bird the easier it is to cook well and, perversely, the cleverer you will be thought.

Few game birds are held in greater esteem by the connoisseur than a roast snipe served on toast as a savoury and yet none could be easier to prepare. You can pluck a snipe in thirty seconds flat. As it is the only game bird which does not have a stomach, it does not even have to be cleaned. Simply stick their long bills up their rear ends and put them under the grill for a few minutes. Just make sure the toast is soaked in a good rich gravy. Cheap port or madeira wine make the best game gravies. Most game birds, however, are best served without sauces. Crisply fried breadcrumbs are the best accompaniment.

Possibly the hardest game bird to cook well is the pheasant. It is the least flavoursome and tends to become very dry if not tended carefully. Personally I find the best liquid to cook it in is gin. Gin brings out its delicate flavour wonderfully.

The greatest sin is to overcook game and particularly grouse. There is a school which claims that grouse should 'be just passed through the flame' but this is rather overdoing it – or rather underdoing it.

By contrast, should it fall to your lot to have to cook a capercailzie, the largest of all our indigenous game birds, it is very difficult either to overcook it or to hang it for too long. Here is a well-tried recipe:

When you have plucked your bird (allow two hours) seal it in a large airtight tin and bury it in the garden for a few weeks. When disinterred, place it in the oven having first stuffed the bird with a very large onion which you will have already peeled and stuck with cloves.

Roast the bird in a slow oven for a further three days, basting it the while in its own juice.

Then take the bird out of the oven, throw it away and eat the onion.

Finally, perhaps the hardest of all game to cook well is venison. Even Mrs Beaton makes a mess of it, which is perhaps why venison has never enjoyed great popularity on the English gentleman's table since the time of the Plantagenets.

All you require to do to make a name for yourself is to cook it along with some oxtail and it will be delicious.

On such small things your reputation as the shooting party hostess will hang and to hell with the sleeping arrangements.

11

Counting the Cost

*I*t is probably true to say that, if the cost is a factor in deciding whether or not to become one of the shooting set, it would probably be better to forget it. Although not quite in the same category as the definition of a really rich man being someone who has no idea of how much he is worth to the nearest few millions it is still necessary to be fairly well-off.

The cost of buying your first gun has already been mentioned. The going price for a pair of guns by a top category gunmaker is very high indeed. William Evans in St James's, for example, will make you a pair for £27,000 and deliver within eighteen months. They will be beautiful guns and a joy for ever. Purdey are generally considered to be at the very top of the league with regard to price. They are also the people to go to if you want optional extras like gold engraving and other indulgences of the mega rich. This sort of thing can push you over the £60,000 mark.

By contrast, it is still possible to buy a second-hand quality gun for anything between £1,000 and £2,000. Spend a further £500 on clothes and equipment like shooting sticks and cartridge bags (not forgetting the leather-bound game book) and you will be able to take your place in the best of company at the covert side.

What a day's sport is likely to cost is something which is nowadays changing with kaleidoscopic speed but the trend continues, as it has done over the last twenty years, to keep on going up ever faster.

Cartridges, which used to cost under sixpence each in old money, now cost ten shillings or £20 for a hundred and everything else has gone up in proportion, including the tip to the head keeper.

The not so long ago days when you might manage to get some fresh air and a shot at a few driven pheasants for a hundred pounds or so are now over, although a few friends can still probably form a small syndicate with a couple of friendly farmers and get their sport for that sort of money.

The more commercially minded syndicates work it out on the cost of putting the birds over the guns. Currently this works out at around £13 a bird. Translated into practical economics, a 200-pheasant day for eight guns will probably cost around £3,000 or more but each gun will get a brace to take home with him. Perhaps a good working figure would be £500 for a decent day per gun.

Grouse shooting will on average cost more for fewer birds. Added to which grouse shooting is an altogether more expensive business in terms of distances to be travelled and the cost of accommodation, like taking a shooting lodge. Much the same applies to deer stalking although the price of a day out on the hill with a stalker can be surprisingly modest.

From all of which it would seem to be the chap who runs the syndicate who is getting all the gravy. Suggest this to him and he will roll his eyes to Heaven, muttering on about feeding and rearing costs, the price of keepering and much, much else besides.

The days when to own an expanse of moor with a few grouse on it was a dubious asset are now, however, long since gone.

The recent purchase by an Arab Sheik of a smallish grouse moor in Yorkshire, which reputedly has a lot of grouse on it, for a figure believed to be in excess of £2,000,000, to which must be added the cost of a large deepfreeze which he has had installed amongst the heather in which to store his surplus birds, just goes to show what a pretty pass we have arrived at.

No you cannot get shooting on the cheap any longer.

Most definitely not.